SNIPERS

SNIPERS

PROFILES OF THE WORLD'S DEADLIEST KILLERS

CRAIG CABELL AND
RICHARD BROWN

JOHN BLAKE

Published by John Blake Publishing Ltd,
3, Bramber Court, 2 Bramber Road,
London W14 9PB, England

www.blake.co.uk

First published in paperback in 2006

ISBN 1 84454 293 9

British Library Cataloguing-in-Publication Data:

A catalogue record for this book is available from the British Library.

Design by www.envydesign.co.uk

Printed in Great Britain by Bookmarque

1 3 5 7 9 10 8 6 4 2

Papers used by John Blake Publishing are natural, recyclable products
made from wood grown in sustainable forests. The manufacturing processes
conform to the environmental regulations of the country of origin.

Every attempt has been made to contact the relevant copyright-holders,
but some were unobtainable. We would be grateful if the appropriate
people could contact us.

'Let's kill him boldly, but not wrathfully.'
CAESAR IN *JULIUS CAESAR* BY WILLIAM SHAKESPEARE

We would like to express our deepest gratitude to James Ravenscroft, our editor at John Blake Publishing, who sadly died at a tragically young age. James, you never saw this book in print but you saw it into print. You completed a first class job and your loss has deeply moved us. A fine man. You will always be in our thoughts.
Richard Brown and Craig Cabell

To Sue and Adam, with love
A special thank you to Colin 'Sid' Ward (ex-Z Troop, 45 Commando) and Paul Greenow (SG8), both good friends.
Richard Brown

To Anita, Samantha, Nathan and Fern, with love
A special thank you to the professional peacekeeping snipers of Great Britain and the USA for your assistance.
Craig Cabell

Authors' Note

We've seen him at the movies as Scorpio in the first *Dirty Harry* film. We've seen him in books, such as Frederick Forsyth's *The Day of the Jackal* and David L Robbins's *War of the Rats*. Some might have experienced him in combat, or even have *been* him in combat. You might even be a loved one affected by sniper action, or just a humble student or punter looking for a different type of read. Well, we can certainly offer you that. In the pages that follow, you will meet assassins, professional soldiers, police officers, chancers, maniacs and, most tragically, victims of snipers.

Why write a book about snipers? Perhaps it's something inherently wrong with that broad thing we call 'society', a supposedly evolving thing that hasn't actually changed as much as one might think over the past 200 years – two centuries since the shot that killed Lord Nelson and gave us the first 'sniper kill' that penetrated public perception and remains in our quite often amnesiac collective conscience. Lord Nelson, like President

Kennedy, ultimately proved that status and power would not protect the individual against the sniper, just as John Lennon failed to survive a maniac shooter's utopia.

The one thing we've learned through writing this book is that the sniper will always terrify society and, chillingly, terrify the populace long after that fatal shot has been fired. We still talk of the deaths of Lord Nelson and President Kennedy and shudder at their cold-blooded murder, but that murder happens in combat all the time. Why are we not so appalled at the brutal wars displayed on our TV screens during the early-evening news? Because our heroes are fighting for good? Because they're playing by the Queensberry rules? Because they can be seen and give the enemy a sporting chance of survival? Dream on. We use snipers too, as you'll see. War isn't polite; it's messy and bloody. Terrorists destroy themselves as readily as they destroy their innocent victims.

We've written this book to provide a glimpse inside the mind of a killer: the sniper. Whether his intentions are good or bad, the sniper still kills from the shadows, and it is this facet of his being that we discuss here. Let's be brutally frank here: there's nothing glamorous about sniper action. It exists as a no-nonsense solution to a problem. And many people have many problems.

Yes, this book deals with well-documented sniper action, but, as Frederick Forsyth explains in his foreword, sniping was happening in a primitive sense long before the advent of the rifle. We simply put a stake in the ground in order to analyse the contemporary sniper and the evolution of sniper action without digging too deeply into the more tenuous and less well-documented areas of history.

One person who didn't quite demand a chapter to himself was Lord Greville Brooke. Born in 1608, Brooke quickly carved his name in the history books as an ardent Puritan and tenacious supporter of Parliament. He refused to join the King's Scottish campaign (1639–40) and as a consequence was imprisoned, but as Lord Lieutenant of Warwick and Staffordshire he fought one of the earliest battles of the English Civil War, in August 1642, against Lord Northampton at Kineton. As commander of Parliament's Midlands Association, he drove the Royalists out of Stratford in February 1643, pushing into Lichfield, where he lost his life, killed by a Royalist sniper stationed on the central tower of Lichfield Cathedral. It was a hell of a good shot, especially considering the weaponry used in those days, but the reason for this digression is to illustrate that Brooke's death, although appearing to be the cause of classic sniper action, cannot be analysed as far as the specifics are concerned – windage, distance, type of gun, etc (well, actually we have a shrewd idea of the latter).

This book has a specific agenda:

a) to analyse sniper action today through a 200-year evolution;
b) to explain the nuances of famous sniper shots and dispel the rumours that have accreted around them over time;
c) to break down the myths surrounding snipers and show the more professional (i.e. soldierly) aspects;
d) to show the need of snipers in today's security services.

The sniper has notoriously lived and worked in the shadows. This book presents the sniper in his various guises.

At this point, it's again appropriate to thank all those members of the security services who helped in its creation. While making an effort to keep the book as realistic as possible, for obvious reasons we've chosen not to disclose any details of recent operations that have included UK and/or US peacekeeping forces.

Craig Cabell and Richard Brown,
London

Foreword
Death in Silence By Frederick Forsyth

For any student of warfare, the sniper has always held a certain chilly fascination. Among all those who bring death to the enemy, he is unique in equipment, psychology and *modus operandi*. When he is bad at his job, he is quickly dead; when he is brilliant at it, he is the battlefield's most deadly killer.

For most of history, men who killed other men saw themselves do it. Even the archer could see his prey fairly clearly. The non-archer had to close to personal combat, to look in the face of the foe, to see the expression in the eyes as the steel went in, to hear the scream, to be sprayed by blood.

After the advent of the musket, the distance between the killer and killed began to lengthen, but even at carbine range the victim was at least visible and the expression on the face of the victim at the moment of death still discernible.

Today the battlefield appears much more to be some kind of weird board game played by remote control. The artilleryman, tank gunner and mortarman cannot really see the damage done; for the fighter and bomber pilot, the victim is way beyond the range of the human eye; for the launcher of rocket and cruise missile, the victims might not even be in the same country.

Hand-to-hand combat is becoming a rare thing, though it is known that at Tora Bora the SAS eventually had lethal recourse to their K-bar knives, and in southern Iraq British soldiers were actually driving in the bayonet, so close and lethal was the fighting with the fanatics. But still they could count on the blazing adrenaline rush, the churning chemical that blinds one to fear and pain for the vital moments.

Not so the sniper. He falls – and always has fallen – between both categories. He might be half a mile from his target but he can see every expression on the face, every gesture, every scowl or yawn, the flash of teeth in a smile, the forkful of food going to the mouth, just before all is ended in death.

He can never, like the gunner, be too far to see anything; he must see everything. But not for him the rush of blood, the war cry, the heat of action, the cut and thrust, the slightly crazed excitement that blankets the human feelings. He alone of those who see the enemy close up must remain ice cold, devoid of passion, a stranger to pity, a workman, a mechanic, a killing tool that cannot allow itself to take surrender instead of death.

There are three aspects that make up the sniper's trade and thence the man himself. First, he must be a marksman of the sort of skill that wins Olympic medals, possessing such an empathy with his weapon that man and tool are fused into a single instrument that will not miss.

Second, because the job might involve crawling for miles to find the ideal firing position, and then up to several days spent motionless in lie-up, he must have awesome patience and stamina or be himself spotted far from home and finished.

And, third, he must have the mindset of one who so completely believes in what he is doing that he can leave the kindly family man far behind him and become an ice-cold implement of someone else's death.

If he can do all of these things, he becomes truly deadly, for his trade is practised, motionless and in silence. Before, during and after the shot, no one will see or hear him. Scanning the area from which the shot came with binoculars will not reveal him, so skilful is his camouflage. All the man who stood beside the corpse knows is that someone is staring at him, two eyes lost in a mass of distance, grass, leaves, paint. All he can do is dive for cover before the second shot takes him too.

Given the cost of modern warfare, the sniper is fearsomely cheap and efficient. One shot, one kill, as the film *Sniper* observed. At that rate, a sniper can theoretically waste a whole battalion with a single box of bullets. Only when he is himself pinpointed is he in serious danger, for he usually has no support and may be far from back-up.

In my first novel, *The Day of the Jackal*, I had my killer as a sniper, but the Jackal's task was easy – to hit a human head, with sniperscope, at 200 yards. Any sniper would expect to take four times that distance and hit the bullseye time after time.

In urban or rural theatres, snipers have been known to kill well over 100 enemy soldiers and still survive without a scratch, something almost impossible for the infantryman.

There are now many bringers of death that are never seen by the victim, but still only one who, himself unseen, stares and squints and fires once, in silence. And he must surely be the battlefield's most fearsome warrior.

Frederick Forsyth
Hertfordshire

Acknowledgements

We would like to thank the National Maritime Museum, the Royal Navy Library (Great Scotland Yard and Portsmouth), the Imperial War Museum, the Army Museum, Frederick Forsyth, David L Robbins and the professional men and women of the military and civil service who gave their time and insight, including unsung heroes who wish to remain anonymous.

Special thanks go to Charles Moose, Emma Noble, *Soldier* magazine, Bantam Press, Orion Books and Andrew Chrysostomu. Thanks to Dave Lakin (aka Zamrok) for his help.

Contents

Introduction

By Richard Brown

On a warm September evening, in a gothic-horror theme
pub in London named the Black Widow, *Snipers* was
born. Craig and I were both staying in the capital during
our attendance at an exhibition and we had arranged to
enjoy one of our very few free evenings over a beer with a
friend from the RAF. Shortly after arriving at the pub, we
learned that our RAF friend had been unavoidably delayed
due to a heavy work load. We looked at one another and
realised that we had a long evening to pass under the
unwavering gaze of a large fake gargoyle. Nevertheless,
good pals as we are, we approached the evening with
stoicism and a stiff upper lip.

As the night passed, we consumed several beers and soon
began to talk about the great topics of conversation that only
ever come up as the beer flows and the wee small hours
approach. On this particular evening, they were, in order:
UFOs, Area 51, Clint Eastwood, John Carpenter films and the

assassination of John Fitzgerald Kennedy. And that's where the conversation took an unexpected swerve.

The analysis of JFK's shooting took a full pint of beer, and then another. It was a topic of unexpected mutual interest, not just because we were both firearms enthusiasts (and all firearms enthusiasts like to discuss the Mannlicher Carcano Oswald used) but also because we both had our own theories, which turned out to be very similar. Of course, these theories did not fall remotely in line with official history, and before long the basis of the Kennedy chapter in this book was written (albeit in our heads), and yet written from a different view: we didn't care who had shot the President; we were interested in *how* the sniper(s) had achieved his (or, indeed, their) objective. We thought about how we would do it, had we been there in 1963. Then we stopped and looked at one another. Our theory would work. Ballistically, it was a runner. To put it another way, we couldn't miss.

Where there's a chapter, there's a book. Before long, we were knee-deep in the world's great sniper tales.[1] I've always been fascinated by snipers and their weapons. It comes from having been an ardent shooter for as long as I can remember. The longer you shoot, the more you try to push distance out of a gun. It's a natural progression. The problem was, where could we go from there?

Then Nelson came out of the blue like a speeding round. This was probably the world's first true sniper shot (a dubious honour for the target!). We realised that no one had ever written about the death of Nelson from this angle. This really was something new.

---

1. The verb *to snipe* derives from the old British sport of shooting Indian snipe birds, which moved very fast and were hard to hit. Gents would go out for a spot of sniping as a sport.

Then there was the Great War. We were on a roll by now and within a week two sample chapters had been written. With Craig's background as an historian and already successful author and my alleged skills as a shooter and amateur writer, combined with our mutual interest in firearms, we felt we could really do something here.

But why did we feel the need to write this book? Primarily because we wanted to read it. There are very few good books on snipers available; indeed, there are very few sniper books out there and, while those that have been written are well read by interested parties, we wanted to create something different: a work of non-fiction that would hopefully act as a good reference book but that would also be an enjoyable read, which historical textbooks so often are not. This is not a technical firearms book, nor are any chapters in it works of fiction (with the exception of Mr Cabell's wonderful short story). Instead, we've taken some of the most notorious sniper shots and sniper scenarios in history, looked at them from a different angle and, we hope, shed new light on some. Most chapters were written on a 'this one's yours, this one's mine' basis, while some we wrote together. All were a pleasure to do.

In the creation of this book, we've been lucky to have generous assistance from many experts on military and historical matters, as well as contributions from two of the world's greatest authors. Many other people have also kindly given their time (and guns!) for us to use. Like a growing child, *Snipers* has metamorphosed and changed as we learned more and as new scenarios came to light. As we researched both the technical and historical aspects of the book, we uncovered some facts that were certainly new to us and will most likely be new to you, too.

While recently visiting Washington, DC, with my wife, I

saw a wonderful T-shirt that I now wish I'd bought. The graphic on the back was simple, just a sniper crosshair, underneath which were the words 'SNIPER – Don't bother to run, you'll just die tired'.

We hope you enjoy this journey into the deadly world of the sniper. We certainly don't want you to finish the book and then feel the need to look over your shoulder... but, then again, there wouldn't be any point. You can't see him. He's too far away.

Richard Brown
London

CHAPTER ONE

What Is A Sniper?

'The average rounds expended per kill with the M16
in Vietnam was 50,000. Snipers averaged 1.3 rounds.
The cost difference was $2,300 v 0.27 cents.'
SIGN HANGING ON THE WALL OF THE USMC SNIPER SCHOOL

*The breathing is controlled; the heart rate is slowed. Tension
is applied to the trigger. The target sits unsuspecting at a
considerable distance. There is no wind to affect the flight of
the round and the sun is from behind. The prone shooter
breathes in deeply, exhales, breathes in again and exhales
while putting gentle pressure on the 3lb trigger.*

*The rifle muzzle cracks and the weapon bounces softly
back into his shoulder. An impossibly small lead projectile
hurtles out of the gun, spinning at high velocity. Forty metres
away, a tin can pirouettes and topples over with a neat entry
hole and a savage rent where the .22 airgun pellet has cut
through the metal and exited.*

This is most people's first experience of scoped rifle shooting. The satisfaction of hitting an object with pinpoint accuracy at a range far greater than the human eye can judge cannot be underestimated, especially at an early age. There is something primal about firing a long-range gun. Perhaps it's the hunter-gatherer in us coming to the surface. Fifteen hundred years ago, our ancestors taught their children to be accurate with a bow and arrow, to be able to kill from such a distance that the target couldn't sense you. This was an essential survival skill to humans in the past, who would starve if they were unable to kill game before it knew they were there. And, of course, there was the deeply held belief that you had to protect your family.

With a long-range weapon, you have the edge over the incoming danger, be it wild animals or invading enemy warriors. Small arms, on the other hand, evoke strange reactions in humans. There is often a sense of fear and uncertainty, there is sometimes a sense of power, but almost always there is a compelling need to pick up the weapon and cradle it. No matter what your personal beliefs are in the good or bad brought by small arms, if you leave a weapon in a room with a collection of randomly selected people, before long someone will pick it up. It is a fact. There is a fascination with this small metal object that can give an individual so much power over his fellow men. If you place the innocent tin can at the bottom of the garden, bring out a good-quality air rifle and then proceed to train the young to shoot, before long all the adults want a go and you have the making of a fine afternoon where parents and children can bond, learning an art that's as old as our species.

But what if the proposed target is human and the shooter must be efficient and calm in a lethal environment? Here we need not simply a good shot; we require the services of a skilled professional who has the coldness of an unfeeling killer and the discipline of a target shooter. We need a sniper.

The role of the sniper carries a degree of kudos in the public eye. He is seen as the lone killer, stealthy, camouflaged, at one with his weapon. He has autonomy where the foot soldier must follow orders. He is a surgical killer who can dominate a battlefield – although, surprisingly, this method of warfare has continually been shunned by military top brass and historically is underutilised.

The sniper is often perceived as a loose cannon. If he is to operate effectively, he requires too much freedom for senior military staff, and so there is the ever-present debate over the added value of one man with one gun.

Let's draw our attention again to the aforementioned sign on the wall of the USMC Sniper School. The arguments against snipers are spurious. Theoretically, one man, with a single-shot weapon and only one bullet, should be able to hold at bay 100 aggressive men. How can this be? Although they could easily collectively overpower him, no individual wants to make the first move. No one wants to be the recipient of that one bullet. Of course, once the sniper has fired this bullet, he'll be overcome by the angry mob, but would you be the first to run at him? One hundred men held at bay by one man, one gun and one bullet. In a world of fully automatic armaments, it pays not to underestimate the power of a single round.

Despite this rather fanciful example, the methodology of sniping holds true. Never in military history has one man with one gun had such dominance over a battlefield. Entire units of crack troops have been halted by a few well-placed, highly disciplined snipers.

So what makes a good sniper? To answer this question fully, we need to analyse three separate elements of the package:

1. The person;
2. The rifle;
3. The tactics.

This is probably the best order in which to discuss these criteria, as each leads to the next. If one fails at any stage, there's no point in moving on to the next element; the structural integrity has gone. Equally, should any of the three elements become substandard during an operation, the end product – the sniper – will be either withdrawn or killed.

In basic survival training, we're taught about the fire triangle. This covers the three key ingredients of a fire:

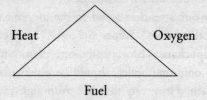

Should one of the sides fail at any point, the triangle collapses and the fire is snuffed out. Anyone who has wrestled with bushcraft will have been there and spent many a cold minute blowing on embers to reignite an extinguished flame.

We can employ the same simple graphical representation and methodology to the sniper:

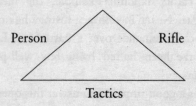

The Person

Snipers have a reputation for being a little odd. It's not that snipers are particularly odd people, it's just that their MO – that of the unilateral killing machine – has never sat particularly well with military doctrine. Anyone who has the capability and the opportunity for independent thought is a potential danger and can wreck a holistic plan.

Even though a sniper might well be teamed up with a spotter, who will be more lightly armed with an assault rifle and binoculars, he is still seen as a loner. And, although he must have an excellent understanding of current military operations, the sniper isn't out on the field with the other troops. In truth, many of his brothers in arms won't know where he is. Of course, geographically the sniper is there, but he is remote from his fellow soldiers.

Some circles believe the sniper's role to be a soft option, a relatively safe position far away from the massed ranks charging machine-gun posts, but nothing could be further from the truth. The sniper's life is a hard one. He is not ensconced safely away from the battle. Indeed, it is quite the opposite. He may be the soldier who is the deepest behind enemy lines, living off his wits and bushcraft skills. He is constantly on the edge, weighing up the pros and cons even before moving to another position, let alone pulling the trigger. The sniper's shot is the calm before the storm. After the crack of his rifle, he can expect the area he's in to be strafed with automatic fire and light weapons. And, just before he pulls the trigger, he will feel fear. Will his muzzle flash be seen? Is his scope reflecting the sunlight? He looks over his shoulder again. Does he have an escape route? Then, of course, there's the deafening noise of the gun. Will the very tool of his trade betray his position?

The sniper is alone with all these fears. He does not have an easy life.

So what makes people want to become snipers? What could attract someone to such a dangerous job? It can be argued that a sniper is actually embracing a regular soldier's greatest fear: that of being alone on the battlefield. To most men in uniform, this would be a frightening prospect, but the sniper is someone who thrives on it. His anonymity and solitary existence – like that of a deep-cover secret agent – are necessary to his own survival.

Is it perhaps a desire for dominance? Having the power of life and death over a target 1,000m away is indeed a strong sensation. Like the aforementioned hunter in the Dark Ages who had to stalk his prey in order to be sure that his arrow would kill, the sniper feels the same rush of adrenaline when he places his Sword-of-Damocles crosshairs on a target nearly a kilometre away.

Perhaps it's his sheer distance from the target, the skill required to fire a projectile over 1,000m, that gives the sniper his 'purpose'. The sixth-century bowman and the sniper with a 7.62mm rifle are both hunters. They have the power to give or take life in an instant.

Power isn't just about the taking of human life. The sniper has the ability to bring absolute chaos to a unit of highly trained enemies by simply shooting an unsuspecting soldier in the middle of the pack or by eliminating the officer as he proudly walks ahead of his men. Suddenly the road ahead has been transformed from an innocuous transit route into a death trap. The squad halts and stares in disbelief at the shattered remains of the officer who had been leading them until only moments ago. Then instinct and training cut in. The squad moves immediately into a well-rehearsed defensive position and begins to lay down suppressing fire in the direction of the incoming shot. But they are too late. The sniper has left via a good exit route and is already slipping away to position number two. And then the second sniper opens up – from the rear. The chaos is multiplied.

Perhaps the prospective sniper simply wants to have every possible advantage over his enemy. He does not care for the fair fight. He is more than happy to be concealed far away from the enemy and shoot with the minimum chance of being shot at. This isn't to imply that the sniper is a coward; indeed, far from it. The sniper is a survivalist, a creature who wants to increase exponentially his chances of staying alive in the field of war. He embraces total concealment but wants to deliver high lethality with complete surprise. More than likely, he will be a man who doesn't naturally like to rely on others. He is a self-sufficient individual who has total confidence in his own abilities.

But don't think that the sniper's role is without danger. The autonomy of a sniper brings danger itself. Often there is genuinely no one to support him. To kill a lonely soldier at 400m is, to the trained shooter, easy enough, but what if the target is a high-ranking military officer who is surrounded by close-protection troops carrying fully automatic weapons? The crack of a rifle will bring a wall of hot lead in his direction – not the easiest thing in the world to escape from. The temptation is to break and run as soon as the rounds are incoming, but that will almost certainly give your position away. A sniper must withdraw slowly. Even as enemy fire is tearing the trees around you to shreds, you must leave calmly and with the minimum of movement. The chances are that the enemy doesn't know where you actually are and the hail of fire will move on to another area. Stealth is your best defence against incoming fire.

You might think that the answer would be to use a suppressed rifle (often incorrectly referred to as a silenced weapon), but this brings its own problems. Trained protection officers will have a good idea where a hostile round has come from, and a suppressed weapon is less accurate than a conventional gun. Suppression works by trapping the very gases that propel the bullet, bleeding them off, inch by inch, along the length of the suppressor. Your gun might be quieter when the bullet finally emerges from the muzzle, but your effective range has been greatly reduced.

One word that articulates what drives a sniper is 'freedom': the freedom to select targets at will and move when he wants to; equally, the freedom to stay where the game is good, the freedom to use non-regulation equipment, the freedom to stamp your individuality on a military role and maybe history – if your target is big enough.

A sniper is free to choose his look. No one sniper's ghillie suit (see annexe B, 'Non-shooting Skills and Kit') can be camouflaged for all environments. He must adapt his look. Be it jungle or urban, he must be a master of environmental disguise. He is, by nature, non-regulation. However, the ghillie suit is just one part of his specialist inventory, which is analysed and catalogued later in the book.

First, though, what of his main piece of equipment?

The Rifle

This instrument forms the second side of our triangle. Fundamentally, it is the sniper's rifle that differentiates him from a foot soldier. Within its niche in the pantheon of firearms, the sniper's rifle is as good as it gets. Most modern sniper rifles have a price tag of around £5,000. For this amount of money, you'll be equipped with one of the finest pieces of military equipment ever invented.

But the modern sniper rifle is a lot more advanced than its predecessors. For many years, snipers operated with 'accurised' standard military rifles. During the Second World War, the British adapted to .303 calibre the classic No. 4 Enfield. This was a proven rifle, being a variant of the bolt-action SMLE (Short Magazine Lee-Enfield), which served the British Army so well during the Great War. Unlike the United States, Britain didn't adopt semi-automatic weaponry for the Second World War but preferred to stay with a bolt-action, manually operated gun, as there was an assumption that the bolt-action mechanism created better shots. It supposedly taught the soldier the benefit of the considered, well-aimed shot, as opposed to the spray-and-pray shooting of a semi-automatic rifle.

This was pure nonsense. Good training with a semi-automatic weapon teaches the shooter not to pull the trigger as fast as he can but to take care over every shot. At least with a semi-automatic weapon he has the option to lay down rapid shots if the situation demands it.

Although this book is not about standard infantry rifles, it is interesting to note that UK forces in the Falklands conflict finally did carry semi-automatic rifles, but by that time all other forces were moving to fully automatic weapons in smaller calibres. Again, UK forces were years behind the rest of the world in small-arms technology. There were even alleged cases of UK troops in the Falklands disposing of their 7.62mm semi automatic L1A1-SLR rifles and carrying stolen Argentine fully automatic weapons. Today's UK military rifle, the SA80, was rushed out because there was such a demand for UK troops to have fully automatic 5.56mm weapons. In true UK military fashion, the SA80 is a very heavy beast that seems to enjoy few of the benefits of the polymer revolution that other armed forces have embraced.

Although accurised guns were adequate tools for early snipers, a purpose-built sniper rifle was always on the cards. Early true sniper rifles often had elements in common with infantry guns, but they were very different creatures from their battlefield counterparts. The British L4A1 was, underneath, a Lee-Enfield rifle re-calibred for 7.62mm – an excellent weapon, and one that remained in UK military service until the 1980s. On such guns, barrels were made specially and actions were either created from scratch or tuned to perfection.

Today, the modern sniper rifle has changed little in principle from those of the 1940s. Despite the hi-tech appearance of some guns, the basic principles of the sniper rifle are the same:

- they are equipped with supremely accurate, purpose-built barrels;
- they have a calibre with sufficient hitting power at long range;
- they're capable of taking a good scope;
- they have a free-floating barrel that is not affected by minor expansions or contractions in the wooden or plastic framework;
- they have a very quiet mechanism;
- finally, in true military techno-talk, they should be 'ruggedised'.

It's interesting to note that this last criterion separates military sniper rifles from police marksman rifles. Although both types of rifle look very similar, and will indeed perform equally well, the police rifle doesn't have to withstand the abuse that a military rifle must suffer. The most harsh environment a police rifle will face is hard rain, whereas military-specification sniper rifle might have to operate at the crack of dawn, at −20°C, after a soldier has carried it through combat for several weeks.

There are many arguments for using either bolt-action or semi-automatic, and this matter is discussed in some detail in annexe A, 'Sniper Rifles and Ammunition'.

Whatever mechanism it uses, a well-built sniper rifle is the most important tool the sniper has. This is perhaps an obvious statement, but the truth is that the world has seen some very average sniper rifles that have not helped the owner to perform his duties. During the Second World War, the mechanism on German Mauser 98K sniper rifles froze in the harsh Russian winter, whereas the indigenous Russian rifle, the Mosin Nagant, was designed with the Russian winter in mind.

Having little faith in your weapon is a terrible state of affairs. So many times in history soldiers have gone into battle with false confidence in their weapons and died as a result. One of the worst cases of this was the ubiquitous M16 in Vietnam. Hailed as a low-maintenance rifle, it soon jammed on the poor GIs, many of whom were killed as a result. A good rifle doesn't make a good soldier, but it certainly helps, as demonstrated in a very clever advertising campaign once used by Colt. The advert showed an American law-enforcement officer pulling his weapon, ready to shoot, while the slogan read: 'A million things can weigh down your mind at this moment. Lighten the load!' The rationale behind the campaign was that being confident in the functioning of your gun is one less thing to worry about. Never has a truer word been said.

Tactics

Now that the correct person has been selected and he or she has the right tool for the job, what do you do with them? The sniper package is a highly valuable asset and must be sensibly deployed.

The worst thing a sniper can do is shoot at a target unworthy of his skills. To risk giving away his position to a foot soldier would be extremely unwise. A sniper must develop patience and master the difficult skill of lying for hours with his eye pressed to the scope. Only when a worthy target appears, and the circumstances for a shoot are correct, should he even consider pulling the trigger.

When confronted with a small unit of men, he should take a long, close look at them and assess each safely from a distance.

Who is the officer? Is there a soldier with a light machine gun who should immediately be target number two? If left alive too long, a machine-gunner – if present – can pose a serious risk, having greater firepower and range than his colleagues. Is there a radio operator? If so, shoot him third and the unit of men is isolated from long-range communications and therefore, potentially, unable to call for support. Finally, do you take out the medic? There is no room for sentiment here; the sniper is effectively looking to destroy the unit's entire command and control structure.

Machines can also make up a substantial part of the sniper's target portfolio. Well-placed high-velocity rounds can do immense damage to military hardware. Take, for example, a multi-million-dollar attack helicopter, bristling with fearsome firepower and the most sophisticated tracking and surveillance equipment – the ultimate war machine. Get a sniper within 1,000m and he can place an anti-material, .50-calibre round into the rotor hub, grounding the helicopter and turning it into a £40 million hunk of metal.

Similarly, there are significant weak points also in tracked vehicles. During combat, no senior officer or driver of a tank or armoured personnel carrier wishes to operate his vehicle while looking out of his hatch. Instead, such vehicles have periscopes or similar devices that allow the crew to see outside while remaining in their steel shell. A sniper can ruin such a scope with a single shot, forcing the tank commander or driver to remain in the open – an unenviable position, when you know it was a sniper who shattered the periscope. Are you next?

Not only can the sniper be used as a weapon of terror, but he is also a valuable intelligence-gathering machine. He has already been trained in stealth and concealment and has highly developed powers of observation. Give him secure communications and his value effectively doubles.

One important question is, what *was* a sniper? In today's military world, the sniper is an enigma. He flies in the face of everything the modern world of combat has embraced – viz automated death from unmanned machines controlled by laptop-equipped soldiers hundreds of miles away. The sniper is a survivor, for, despite our frightening advances in weaponry, he is still one of the most powerful elements on the battlefield. Like no other conventional weapon, he can strike fear into the very soul of a soldier. He causes panic and confusion on such a significant level that he can fundamentally unbalance an entire unit of men. As a result, today there is a fascination about snipers.

This book takes a fresh look at some of the greatest snipers and sniper shots in history and seeks to understand why they maintain such a hold on our psyche, and what they've individually brought to the world of sniping.

Supremely accurate weapons aren't unique to the twentieth and twenty-first centuries, as discussed in the early chapters of this book, which cover the world of sniping of the eighteenth and nineteenth centuries. However, one of the world's great guns was patented on 5 October 1852, when Christian Sharps unveiled his now legendary Sharps Carbine .50-calibre rifle, which would one day arm the US Seventh Cavalry and, in civilian hands, see the end to thousands of American buffalo. An unknown owner of one of these superb rifles delivered a quote that admirably sets the tone for the rest of this book: 'If I can see it, I can kill it!'

CHAPTER TWO

Saratoga – The Sharpshooter Emerges

'I think we had better move or we shall shortly
have two or three of these gentlemen amusing
themselves at our expense.'

MAJOR G HANGER, WHILE UNDER FIRE FROM
AMERICAN SHARPSHOOTERS

The wars in America have given rise to a number of interesting firearms and tales connected to them. If you want interesting historical stories about small arms, American history is the one to study.

The American Civil War saw the issue of the Colt .36-calibre Navy-model percussion pistol, one of the world's first great revolvers. Originally, its components were fashioned out of wood by a young naval officer, one Samuel Colt, and when it went into mass-production years later the Navy became the backbone of the Colt catalogue in the mid-1800s.

In the 1860s, the Navy model was superseded by the .44-calibre Colt Army, so named because it was issued in large numbers to the Union Army during the Civil War. To this day, the Colt Army is one of the most aesthetically beautiful firearms ever conceived. Its elegant lines and superior build make it a joy to own (although a muzzle-loading gun has no military value in the twenty-first century).

As the brass cartridge came into use, Colt gave us probably the most famous handgun of all time: the Colt Single Action Army, or 'Peacemaker', in .45 Long Colt calibre.

Along with manufacturers like Remington, Smith & Wesson and Winchester, these guns made a nation. However, to discuss one of the most interesting tales concerning muzzle-loading weaponry, we have to go back almost another 100 years, to the American Revolutionary War and, specifically, the Battle of Saratoga.

By 1777, the American Revolutionary War against Colonial occupation was at its bloody height. The war-torn landscape of the New World had already seen some of the great battles that would shape its history – Lexington and Concorde, *inter alia*. In 1776, the Declaration of Independence had been announced and British troops began to fight not only for the land that they believed to be theirs but also, as the war turned, for their very lives.

At this point, the war was still a long way from spiralling out of the control of the British, but the American military – built up of ragtag troops in blue coats and militiamen in working clothes – could feel the tide turning. Every day their numbers swelled and the British tactic of massed rifles was proving unsuitable for the guerrilla fighting of the militias. Future events such as the American–French Alliance of 1778 and Spain declaring war on the British in 1779 would spell the end of British rule, ultimately leading to a humiliating surrender in 1781.

Ironically, it would take another terribly bloody war, a new type of conflict in a new millennium, for a US President to say to a British Prime Minister, 'America has no truer friend than Great Britain. Once again, we are joined together in a great cause. I'm so honoured the British Prime Minister had crossed an ocean to show his unity with America. Thank you for coming, friend.' But such a sea-change in transatlantic relations was still over 200 years in the future.

On 17 October 1777, on the shores of the Hudson River in New York State, there was no love lost been Britain and America. They were the direst of enemies and nothing but the total defeat of one force would end the battle that was to follow.

In order to effect a suppression of the New England colonies, Lord Germaine – the official in the British Government with direct control of the war policy – directed Major-General John Burgoyne and Brigadier Simon Fraser to march their joint British, Canadian and Indian forces from Canada down a route via Lake Champlain, along the Hudson River.

The army was massed and set forth, marching confidently in their red coats and a variety of headgear, depending on the regimental dress code of each division. There were bearskins, making the men look seven feet tall; leather hats; and the famous three-cornered hat, the tricorne – hugely impractical but visually stunning. Along with them marched the German infantry.

Burgoyne and Fraser's first port of call was a fort named Ticonderoga, which they reached on 1 July 1777. The American officer in command of the fort decided that discretion was the better part of valour and fled on sight of the 7,300-strong British lead force. The triumphant 'Red Coats' moved on.

A prime tactic for the American militiamen, who lacked the

skills to fight in massed ranks, was to block off the supply routes to the advancing British forces. Burgoyne foresaw this tactic and, on reaching the area around Skenesboro, he gave the order to clear the road to the north, in order to free up a supply route, and south, to allow for the free movement of his troops.

However, it was here that the combined force lead by Burgoyne suffered a setback. The general sent a colonel, named St Ledger, on a territory-gaining raid along the Mohawk River while he directed some German troops under his command on a foraging exercise to find food. The small German force was overwhelmed by an American force, as was a second detachment of troops sent out to find them. Two senior officers were captured. St Ledger was also persuaded to return to the main force, as he was experiencing difficulties with his local troops, mainly due to the efforts of Native Americans.

The upshot of this sorry affair was that neither the order to find food nor that to free up the south road had been fulfilled. The only result was that the British were now short of two commanders and a number of German troops.

Lacking the regimented training of the British troops (or perhaps the lunacy to stand in ranks and be shot at), the American militiaman had developed their own highly successful tactics, which were a cross between stealth ambushing, sniper work and outright hit-and-run guerrilla warfare – a favoured technique that deployed the natural environment against the British.

The Red Coats had a habit of moving off in the early morning. As was common in the south, this time of day is prone to a heavy mist so thick that it was difficult to see any great distance. The militiamen would first arrange a wall of shooters at a strategic point, within flintlock range, well in advance of the obvious route they suspected the British would use. They would then place lookouts regularly spaced high in trees along this route, above the level of the mist – an early take on the sniper spotter.

Although there was always the possibility that the spotters couldn't actually see the ground beneath them, it was obvious when British troops were passing due to the noise of them marching.

As the enemy passed under each spotter, he would make a silent signal to the next lookout, who would be watching him with either the naked eye or a telescope. The process would then be repeated, and repeated again, to provide a highly effective way of tracking the progress of the enemy and of silently giving advance notice of their route and speed.

The senior officer in charge of the 'shooting wall' would also be equipped with a scope, and his remit was to watch nothing but the very last spotter, waiting for his signal, which was the most important as the final spotter was placed at optimum rifle distance from the waiting shooters. The riflemen of the shooting wall would be aiming directly at the base of his tree. As the final spotter made his pre-arranged 'open fire' signal, the shooters would fire blindly at the target area.

The effect was devastating, and of course the British troops had no idea where the shots had come from. To cause total confusion, other shooters might have been placed at a slightly different shooting angle in order to give the impression of multiple incoming fire from different directions. Having fired possibly only one deadly volley, militiamen scattered and went to ground. The plan was that, with any luck, the British troops would run in all directions and start shooting at one another.

The British forces were in a difficult situation. Burgoyne and Fraser had orders to continue with the advance south, but they had insufficient supplies. Raids by the local militiamen were becoming increasingly common, so remaining *in situ* proved to be equally dangerous. Retreat, of course, was never an option, so the British chose to stay put, defend their position and prepare as best they could for a later push south. It took them until 13 September 1777 to achieve this.

Advancing again, but feeling the effects of countless insurgency raids, Burgoyne and Fraser reached the heavily defended American fort of Bemis Heights. The scene was set for one of the most important battles in the Revolutionary War: the Battle of Saratoga.

The British forces were outnumbered by local soldiers led by General Benedict Arnold. Despite superior numbers in favour of the British, the battle advantage moved alternately between both armies, with highly trained fighting men employing various different tactics on both sides. Each side fought for land that they believed was theirs by God-given right.

Finally, the battle began to swing in favour of the British troops. As the Revolutionary forces were pushed back yet again, the British commanders realised that the initiative had to be seized.

Brigadier Simon Fraser had been instrumental in the success of the British forces. He was a charismatic figure, sitting astride a grey horse, and continually rode in front of his men, encouraging them to advance. He galloped furiously along his advancing front, pushing his men to take advantage of any weakness in the American lines.

Fraser's presence had not gone unnoticed by his American counterparts. Seeing the effect this mounted senior officer was having on the advancing British and German soldiers, General Arnold is reported to have shouted, 'That man on the grey horse is a host in himself and must be disposed of!'

The call was out and Fraser was a marked man. Several crack US soldiers armed with flintlock rifles were despatched to remove the British officer who was proving to be such a catalyst to the advancing army. Dressed in natural colours and skilled at long-range shooting, these eighteenth-century pre-snipers moved out with one high-value target in their sights. One of the shooters was a young man of just twenty-six years. His name was Timothy Murphy.

Murphy was one of the great heroes of the Revolutionary War. There are numerous accounts of his actions in the battle at Bemis Heights, and we will look at some of these in detail later, but for the moment let us take a step back and find out who this man was and how he came to be at the Battle of Saratoga.

Timothy Murphy was born in the Delaware Water Gap area in 1751. As his family name suggests, Murphy's parents were of Irish origin, and moved to Pennsylvania in 1759, settling in the area of Sunbury. As was the trend at the time, young Timothy was given an apprentice job with a wealthy local family. Keen to see more of the country and hungry for adventure, he travelled with this family when they ventured out into the wilds of Wyoming County. This was the frontier, far from civilisation, and it was in this region that Murphy acquired a real hatred for the local Indians, who would frequently raid his homestead. The skills of the frontier – which included long-range shooting – were essential to learn if he was to survive this early life. Skill with a flintlock pistol alone wasn't enough to keep you alive in this dangerous land. If you were close enough to your target to use a pistol, you'd allowed your enemy to get too close and would most likely not have time to reload. If you could engage your target(s) at long range, you might have the opportunity to fire several shots.

In 1775, Murphy enlisted in his local militia, keen to fight the British invaders, and in his new unit he fought at Boston and at the Battle of White Plains. Two years later, he found himself moving to upstate New York with General Daniel Morgan as part of a force despatched to halt the advance of a southbound British Army lead by one Major-General John Burgoyne. The two forces met at Bemis Heights.

On the command to despatch the officer on the grey horse,

Murphy climbed a tree and found a V-shaped notch in the branches that would support the muzzle weight of his rifle. (Bipods and tripods had yet to be invented but, in warfare as in most other things, nature could provide.) At a range of around 300 yards, Murphy cocked his weapon and took a steady aim at the distant British officer on the grey horse. He fired one shot and hit Fraser through his intestines with a lead ball, blasting him off his horse. Indeed, his wounds were so serious that Fraser died the next day. (There are accounts of Murphy firing at least twice before he hit Fraser, although it's more likely that these shots came from other sharpshooters; we know, after all, that several militiamen were after this target.)

Moments after his shooting of Fraser, Murphy spied another senior British officer galloping across the Red Coat line, bearing an important message. Messengers were equally desirable targets for the militia, and so, having established the range of the British soldiers, Murphy took a shot at the rider, Sir Frances Clarke, chief adviser to General Burgoyne. Clarke was dead before he hit the ground.

These two shots shattered British morale. News of Fraser's death spread amongst the troops like a deathwatch beetle in wood. They couldn't believe that a sharpshooter had killed the general from such a range. How many shooters were there? Was it safe for any of them to advance any further?

The timely appearance of another 3,000 American troops was the final turning point in the battle. The British soldiers were now outnumbered three to one, and the inevitable cave-in of their ranks soon followed. 'Sureshot Tim', as Murphy was later dubbed, had earned his place in American history.

But this isn't a book about battles; it's about snipers, and we shall respectfully put aside the events at Saratoga to look at the two shots fired by Murphy and the weapon he might have used.

There are several reports that Murphy was armed with a Goulcher double-barrelled rifle, and this is certainly possible, although there are an equal number of reports which state that Goulcher weapons – which were of Swiss manufacture – were not common in the Revolutionary War. It's far more likely that Murphy was armed with a Kentucky long rifle.

Murphy might even have carried two rifles, knowing full well how long it would take him to reload while dangerously exposed up in a tree. He might also have carried a double-barrelled shotgun for close-range defence, as flintlock versions of these guns were common and could perhaps be mistaken for the Swiss two-shot gun. It could be the case that Murphy later owned a Goulcher, and that this weapon was mistakenly identified as the gun that killed Fraser and Clarke. Whatever the tool, however – and we will never truly know what type of gun he used – the firing principles that Murphy must have observed were the same for all of the aforementioned guns.

Like all personal weapons of this period, Murphy's rifle would have operated on the flintlock principle. It would be almost another decade before the percussion principle would be invented, which would ultimately lead to the introduction of the metallic cartridge.

All flintlock weapons operate on the same fundamental principles, but we will later see that there was a fundamental difference between the weapons used by the British troops at the time of Saratoga and those used the American militiamen.

To fire a flintlock weapon – let's assume it's a Kentucky – a measure of gunpowder is first poured down the long (40–50-inch) barrel. For the American troops, this would most likely have come from a powder flask, which – like a modern sugar dispenser – would deliver a preset measured amount of gunpowder: sufficient to fire a round but not enough to damage the weapon. The shooter would then push wadding down the barrel with his ramrod, which was stored under the barrel and took the form of a long wooden stick with a brass plunger on the end, which fit snugly against the barrel to ensure that all of the propellant (i.e. the gunpowder) was forced to the rear of the gun. Then, a lead ball – at this time, typically between .40-inch and .50-inch calibre, depending on the individual gun – would be pushed down the barrel with the rod. (In order to reduce the amount of time it took them to add the wadding, it's likely that knowledgeable soldiers would have pre-wadded or wrapped their lead balls in grease patches, which would make it much easier to push the ball down into the tight-fitting barrel.) Once the round and its charge were securely at the base of the barrel, the shooter would then turn his attention to the lock at the side of the rifle.

The firing mechanism of a flintlock is comprised of three main parts: the hammer, the frizzen and the priming pan. The hammer looks like a hammer on the side or rear of any gun today but, rather than hitting a modern firing pin, the hammer of a flintlock has two integrated jaws that grip a piece of flint that has been specially shaped for the gun. The frizzen, meanwhile, is an L-shaped piece of metal that folds down to cover the priming pan and moves forward on contact with the falling hammer. The priming pan itself is a small basin at the side of the gun in which a small measure of gunpowder is poured. The ignition of this powder on the outside of the gun will send a flame through a charge hole drilled in the side of the barrel, into the main powder charge. For this small priming charge to be ignited, the hammer is first pulled fully back. (There are two settings for the hammer: full cock and half cock. The gun won't fire on half cock, hence the expression 'going off half-cocked'.) Pulling the trigger then releases the hammer, and as it flies forward the flint hits a flat plate on the frizzen, creating a shower of sparks that should ignite the main charge, weather permitting! (Wind and rain are the worst enemies of the flintlock shooter. Although the frizzen covers the pan, protecting the powder, while the gun is in transit, the instant the hammer hits home, it forces the frizzen forward to allow the resultant sparks access to the small powder charge in the pan. In heavy rain, the pan is instantly soaked. In a gale, the powder can be blown away.)

Assuming that all of the above works, the shooter must then deal with a sizeable and very distracting explosion at the side of his gun. The small charge then hopefully sends a blast through the charge hole and ignites the main charge. There is a time delay between the first blast and the main shot, and only an experienced shooter will be able to stay on target through the priming blast, while waiting for the main charge to fire.

With such an intricate firing mechanism, it's easy to see why two flintlock rifles were often carried, with a double-barrel shotgun and a flintlock pistol serving as back-up.

Another disadvantage of flintlock rifles is the large volume of smoke they create. Once you fire a flintlock, your position is well and truly given away. Only in a battlefield already wreathed in powder smoke will you stand a chance of remaining concealed.

Now that we have a feel for the complex loading system Murphy had to deal with as he sat up in his arboreal vantage point, it's important to look at the flintlock in some detail. Modern shooters who benefit from self-loading guns and box magazines should remember that their ancestors had to fight with much more complex and physically demanding equipment.

Irrespective of what weapon Murphy actually used, it's possible to say with some certainty that, if he was indeed to pull off a shot with a flintlock at a distance of upwards of 300 yards, he most likely had a rifle, as opposed to a musket. The difference here is – as the name implies – that a rifle has a rifled barrel while a musket has a smooth-bore barrel, like those of some modern shotguns. When spin is imparted to a bullet by the rifling in a barrel, the round is far more accurate than a bullet forced down a smooth bore, which is effectively nothing more than a tight-fitting steel tube.

Could this shot have been fired twice, though? We know that at 200 yards the Kentucky weapon was deadly, which is itself a fine boast for a gun of this era; any weapon that can display such accuracy at 200 yards is more than capable of a good level of accuracy over a longer range in the hands of a competent shooter. One of the great pleasures of long-range rifle shooting is in finding the correct level of elevation necessary to push greater and greater ranges out of the gun. A modern sniper sight helps you to do this. As you zero the crosshairs of the scope to the correct position, corresponding with the estimated distance of the target, the rifle is being pointed artificially upwards in order to allow for the gravity-induced curve of the rising and falling round. There's no reason why this can't be executed with the naked eye if the gun is in the hands of a skilled marksman.

So, unquestionably, Murphy could have killed Fraser and Clarke. After all, we do know that Murphy cradled his rifle in a V-shape notch in the tree's branches. By taking the human 'wobble' out of shooting, the accuracy of the gun can be maximised. The gun itself doesn't become any more accurate; it just doesn't shake so much.

Although we can look romantically at the Kentucky today as a wonderful relic of the past, in 1777 it was a formidable fighting tool. So what other characteristics made it the best of its day?

For a start, both the gun and the ammunition were lightweight. Given the environment in which Murphy lived and grew up, most travelling was done on foot. The heaviest item a man would carry was probably his rifle. If this was a dead weight and took large, heavy lead balls, the frontier dweller would have little strength to carry food and water. The Kentucky weighs six pounds, which compares favourably to the Second World War's Lee-Enfield, which tips the scales at around nine pounds. The combination of a good powder flask and a bag of lead balls also weighs less than a belt of modern brass cartridge ammunition.

The gun also had to be quick to load and accurate. Despite the long loading procedure described above, in skilled hands a flintlock weapon can be primed quickly. There are numerous verifiable tales of soldiers being able to load and fire in fifteen seconds, and so firing rates of up to four shots a minute could be achieved. This level of expertise took years of practice, but it was possible, especially if prepared patched balls were used, as mentioned earlier.

Remember that a bullet is always traditionally bigger than the barrel down which it is fired. This is the only way in which all of the charge can be trapped behind the round, thus giving it maximum velocity. Historically, flintlocks were filled with powder and a large lead ball (i.e. .457 for a .45 gun). Often guns were supplied with a small hammer with which to hit the end of the ramrod and force the bullet home. Lead is soft, and this was undoubtedly achievable, but often only with great effort. Considering that some flintlocks peaked at upwards of .70 calibre, with some guns you could find yourself ramming home a very large lump of lead.

The patched ball was a clever concept whereby the lead round was actually slightly smaller than the barrel and was wrapped in a greased patch, making it very easy to ram home. The only problem was that, when the shot was discharged, the wadding burned away and the ball then rattled down the length of the barrel. This shortcoming was quickly addressed, however, by the development of a conical bullet with a hollow base, which expanded as the charge ignited, the skirt of the bullet gripping the barrel's rifling on the way out. This system was so successful that it is still used in air-gun ammunition today. Just enough of the round catches the rifling to impart spin, but most of the lead slug is left unmolested by the rifling's cutting force and maintains a high level of aerodynamics.

Flintlocks are easy guns to maintain. As long as he keeps a supply of ready-shaped flints, some raw lead, a bullet mould and a full powder flask, the shooter is almost self-sufficient. The traditional blowing down the barrel after firing isn't just for show; it removes excess fouling from the charge hole at the lock end of the barrel. And no special tooling is required to maintain a flintlock, as the lockwork has very few moving parts. All in all, this makes for a reliable gun in the wild frontier.

One part of the long rifle's designation is particularly important: the word 'long'. The barrel of the Kentucky, and so many rifles of this era, was indeed very long. Indeed, when measured against the equivalent weapons of today, the Kentucky seems excessively long, making it almost unmanageable. As assault rifles become ever smaller in response to today's military specifications (the Kalashnikov AKSU, for example, is only 16 inches long with the butt folded), at 50 inches long the Kentucky seems archaic. Nevertheless, it works. Indeed, its designers created the gun to give the large black-powder-propelled ball maximum trajectory and speed.

As mentioned earlier, a flintlock creates a great deal of smoke, which begs the question, why didn't the British soldiers simply aim at the spot where Murphy fired and pepper the area with shot?

The problem lay in the fact that the British had inferior firearms. In 1777, the British were still carrying as a standard sidearm the musket flintlock, a paper-cartridge, smooth-bore weapon that peaked in accuracy at a range of around 200 yards. When we consider that Murphy was over 300 yards from his target, and concealed in trees above ground level, we can surmise that he was relatively safe. The British were trained in massed volley firing and weren't skilled marksmen, and so would not have the discipline to take time over complex, long-range shots.

The British flintlock gun was an old weapon that had more in common with guns of the mid-1600s than with any modern weapon approaching the turn of the eighteenth century. It operated on the same flintlock principle as Murphy's gun (whatever that actually was), but as it was a smooth-bore weapon it can't accurately be called a rifle.

The cartridge (around .76 calibre) was quick to load, with the powder charge and lead bullet being contained in a paper tube. The end of the tube was bitten off by the shooter to expose the powder (which tastes foul!), a small measure of which was then poured into the priming pan, after which the frizzen was closed. The gun was then up-ended (first problem) and the remaining powder-and-paper-covered ball rammed down the barrel – an action that becomes progressively harder as the barrel fouls up. The gun was then shouldered and sighted, its hammer cocked, and fired.

The British weapon's operating principles weren't hugely different in function to that of the American guns, but the entire process was backwards. With the British weapon, it was so easy to lose powder out of the priming pan, for instance, that to place powder in there first seems foolhardy. Far better to ram home the load with as much force as needed and then to charge the priming pan. So many times British troops fully loaded their guns to find that, in the loading process, some powder had fallen from the pan and there wasn't enough left to ignite the main charge.

This wasn't the only problem with the paper cartridge. One very unique issue that would plague the British Empire in years to come was the fact that the grease which coated the cartridge (in order to aid loading and to keep the paper dry) was made of the mixture of cow and pig fat, which offended the nineteenth-century British Army's Hindu contingent, who saw the cow as a sacred animal. It also offended British Muslim soldiers, who saw the pig as an unclean creature. Indeed, in February 1857, a local British regiment in India refused to accept the new cartridges and had to be disarmed and disbanded. From a religious standpoint, a worse mix for the grease could not possibly have been created.

Armed with smooth-bore guns and very large, heavy bullets, the British couldn't gain the level of accuracy that made Murphy and his fellow sharpshooters so dangerous. It is, however, possible to shoot accurately enough with a British muzzle-loader of the day; one can place ten individually loaded shots into a 12-inch circle, but this can be done at a range of only around 50 yards! At 100 yards, you'd be lucky to hit a man-sized target. The guns used by the British forces were designed for volley firing, not individual, well-aimed shots. There simply was no comparison between the muskets used by the British Red Coats and the rifle used by Timothy Murphy.

So, was Timothy Murphy a sniper? Perhaps not in the truest sense of the word, but he was without doubt a very good shooter who, in the heat of battle, was capable of pulling off very accurate shooting over excessively long distances. His two famous shots at the Battle of Saratoga created chaos in the ranks of the enemy as two of their senior officers were gunned down at what seemed impossibly long ranges – an accepted sniper tactic.

Skill with a rifle was, in 1777, something to boast about. Today, shooters tend to remain quiet and avoid publicity, but, during the time of the Revolutionary War, a sharpshooter was a hero, someone for the youth of the time to aspire to emulate. Murphy was an innovator.

There are numerous tales of antics with guns, but one well-known story involves a display of shooting by two brothers as they showed off their talents in front of the local populace. One brother was seen to take a piece of wood, which was alleged to be around 5 inches by 7, and nail to the centre of it a piece of paper the size of a playing card. He then gripped the board between his thighs and stood perfectly still. The second brother then loaded his flintlock and walked out to a distance that varies (depending on the storyteller) between 40 and 60 yards. The shooter then proceeded to fire a total of eight lead bullets through the paper, in an outstanding display not only of brotherly faith but of marksmanship. The two brothers then informed the crowd that there were upwards of fifty men in their regiment who could match these feats and better. This was a powerful recruiting campaign for the youth of the day and showed the local people very graphically that the militia was both well armed and well trained.

News of these escapades would have reached the British ears before long, although the tales may have been exaggerated by countless retellings. However, with many men having witnessed their senior commander's intestines being blown out by a distant shooter, the stories must have seemed horribly real.

There are those who will argue that Murphy was not a sniper and has no place in this book, but we have striven to show not only how the modern sniper works but also, historically, from whence his skill comes. Shooting with iron sights (i.e. without a scope) is a pure skill, with man and weapon operating in perfect harmony. The shooter doesn't have the aid of a 4x magnification scope to zero in on the target. There is no artificial help. And let's not forget how small and far away a man and horse look at 300 yards – less than half the height of your little finger.

Timothy Murphy went on to fight in many more battles during the Revolutionary War. Although he didn't take part in the battle, some of his fellow riflemen joined General Washington as he drove the British from Philadelphia. Then, in 1779, Murphy's enlistment time with the riflemen expired and he joined a new company of militia. He was later captured by Indians but escaped with a friend and systematically knifed all of his eleven captors while they slept. It is still debated today who Murphy hated most: the British or the indigenous natives.

While he was with the new militia, Murphy still captured the American imagination with his exploits. On one occasion, he was stranded in a besieged fort with 200 of his riflemen. The fort commander decided to surrender, as he believed that a fight was impossible against the superior number of British soldiers surrounding them. As the commander moved to take down the flag, Murphy fired two warning shots over his head. A tense stalemate in the fort followed, but Murphy attracted loyalty and the commander was confined to quarters with the other occupants of the fort, following Murphy's lead. The siege continued but ended with the British withdrawing, due to the cost of keeping a large number of troops in the area and their inability to approach the camp under the eye of the sharpshooters.

When the war ended, Murphy hung up his rifle and began a life of farming, milling and dabbling in local politics. He died in 1818.

The British learned from the attacks by Murphy's men. Although they took their time, by the turn of the century the British Army was being issued with the excellent new Baker rifle, a weapon that embraced all the outstanding characteristics of the Kentucky in a smaller, more manageable package. Unlike the very long American guns, the Baker rifle (and this was indeed a rifle) had a barrel length of 30 inches. At 200 yards, it was capable of a guaranteed kill shot, while reaching the target from a distance of 300 yards was easily achievable if the shooter could compensate for environmental factors. With a little luck, the new weapon could achieve distances of over 400 yards.

The actions of Timothy Murphy, the sniper of the Battle of Saratoga, had a fundamental effect on small-arms warfare in the eighteenth century, not because of the tool he used but because of his skill with it – his ability to draw on every last inch of the weapon's accuracy at impossible ranges. He fully capitalised on the British habit of dressing the most senior commanders in resplendent uniforms and having them stand proudly, even arrogantly, in front of their troops. Some would argue that this is a commander's place, but when the enemy is as skilled at shooting as the American militia was, something had to change – and change it did, although probably only after the death of Lord Nelson a little over thirty years later, as discussed in the next chapter.

But the British Army did change, instigated largely by the introduction of the Baker rifle. With this new gun came a new soldier who owed much to the *modus operandi* of the old enemy militiamen. Gone was the red coat and white bandoleers. Instead, the new rifle corps wore green and black. For the first time, the British soldier was camouflaged, just as his militia enemy had been so many years before. The new army embraced militia tactics, such as concealment and stealth, and used similar equipment, including pre-patched balls and powder horns.

On a later 1808 recruiting poster for the new Green Jackets, the would-be soldier is informed, 'In this distinguished service, you will carry a rifle no heavier than a fowling piece. You will knock down your enemy at five hundred yards instead of missing him at fifty. Your clothing will be green…'

Thirty one years earlier, this poster could well have been describing the Saratoga sniper, Timothy Murphy, whose innovations and sharp shooting have earned him a place in this book and in military history.

CHAPTER THREE

The Death of Lord Nelson

'Engage the enemy more closely.'
LORD NELSON'S LAST SIGNAL

Lord Nelson died on 21 October 1805 at approximately 1630hrs. He lived long enough to hear that the greatest sea battle ever fought was his, but he died from a sniper wound received in the height of battle at 1315hrs.

Who was the sniper? What was his weapon? How accurate was the weapon? Where did he shoot from? What obstacles stood in his way? Did he deliberately set out to kill Lord Nelson?

It is our firm belief that the shot which killed Lord Nelson was one of the world's first true sniper shots, and like all truly successful sniper shots – such as that which killed President Kennedy – there is an air of mystery that surrounds it. So let's travel back 200 years and peer through the gunsmoke and carnage to view the circumstances and logistics of that famous shot and discover if it was really one man, one bullet, or some other reason that makes it the world's first true sniper shot.

The Battle of Trafalgar was the most significant sea battle of the nineteenth century. Lord Nelson's fleet was outnumbered by the combined fleets of France and Spain, commanded by Admiral Villeneuve, but, owing to a revolutionary strategy entitled 'The Nelson Touch', victory was achieved by the British without a single ship lost. However, it was The Nelson Touch that put HMS *Victory* (Lord Nelson's flagship) in mortal danger of capture.

The manoeuvre meant splitting the British fleet into two columns, which would sail at right angles to the enemy line of battle, one heading for the centre and the other for the rear. Although this effectively segregated the French from the Spanish, close-quarter fire was inevitable. It was here that HMS *Victory* was nearly lost. But, as Turner's famous painting *The Fighting Temeraire* depicts, the *Temeraire* came to Lord Nelson's aid.

HMS *Victory* broke from the *Bucentaure* and engaged with the *Redoubtable*. Nelson, with his usual disregard of personal safety, was commanding the fighting of his men from the quarterdeck. He had been warned on many occasions to hide his decorations, but always refused. (Sir Thomas Hardy reputably advised him at Trafalgar to do so but the request was refused.) [2]

Lord Nelson was therefore a prime target. He gave his orders from the quarterdeck and, at 1.15pm on 21 October 1805, an unknown 'sniper' took aim from the *Redoubtable* and shot his Lordship through the shoulder. Nelson was mortally wounded. [3]

---

2. Some people have speculated that Lord Nelson wanted to die at Trafalgar, which is why he wore his medals. This is quite untrue. Hardy had had similar arguments with his Lordship regarding such vanity as wearing his decorations. The background to the 'death-wish' scenario is basically due to the fact that Nelson's sight was beginning to go in his left eye – which would ultimately make him completely blind – and he allegedly suffered pain from the stump of his right arm and an old wound to his side.

This is the legendary story of the death of Lord Nelson, but during the 200 years since his demise many variations on it have been created. One conspiracy theory is that Nelson was shot by his own men before the battle started. This is, of course, sheer nonsense. Nelson's men respected him greatly; he was quite a lenient leader, so there was no question of him being killed by his crew as a result of a grudge, potential mutiny or even accident.

But what about the possibility that Nelson was shot from the enemy's deck? As a hypothesis, this cannot be ruled out, but it's not actually the way it happened, as is confirmed by certain evidence that will soon be discussed. Yes, a shot could enter his shoulder and deflect down through his body, but this in fact did not occur.

The French posted snipers in the rigging of their ships – a tactic eschewed by the British, who feared that they could thus set their own sails alight. In the foreground of Denis Dighton's painting of Nelson, there is a Marine clearly firing directly up into the enemy's rigging. But can we believe the artistic licence of a painter? No, we can't. Instead, we visited the Royal Navy Archive and read a first-hand account of the event by Nelson's surgeon, Sir William Beatty.

Beatty presented us with a wealth of evidence to prove that Lord Nelson was shot from the Mizzen top of the *Redoubtable*, and not just eyewitness reports but medical evidence, too.

3. By 1805, the long-arm had undergone a revolution. It had become the rifle. Smooth-bore barrels were suddenly old technology. Now, weapons had rifled barrels, which delivered a high-velocity, spinning round. The rifle used by Nelson's killer would have been, for its day, an advanced weapon. As discussed in the previous chapter, a smooth-bore flintlock can achieve consistent shots in a 12-inch circle at about 25–30 yards. With a rifled barrel, this level of accuracy can be extended to 100 to 200 yards. The famous Baker rifle even claimed to be capable of this tight grouping at 300 yards. HMS *Victory* was well within the accurate range of *Redoutable* riflemen.

However, as we will clearly show, the 'sniper shot' that killed Lord Nelson was not that professional.

The evidence to support this claim is presented in the second edition of Beatty's *The Death Of Lord Nelson: 21 October 1805* by William Beatty, MD, Surgeon of HMS *Victory*. [4]

On 11 December 1805, with Lord Nelson's body still aboard HMS *Victory*, Beatty wrote the following:

> Doctor Beatty's Professional Report at sea, HMS *Victory*...
> Lord Nelson was mortally wounded in the left breast by a musket ball, supposed to be fired from the Mizzen top of *La Redoubtable*, [a] French ship of the line, which the *Victory* fell on board of early in the Battle. His Lordship was in the act of turning on the quarter-deck with his face towards the enemy when he received his wound. He instantly fell and was carried to the Cockpit, where he lived about two hours.

It's a pretty loose description of what happened, particularly when, elsewhere in the book, Beatty reveals that it took Lord Nelson two hours forty-five minutes to die, instead of the stated two hours, and, more importantly, Nelson's fatal wound was received through his left shoulder, not through his left breast. Not only is this confirmed by an inspection of Nelson's coat, displayed in the National Maritime Museum in Greenwich; it is also confirmed by Beatty elsewhere in his book!

However, in Beatty's 'autopsy' report, he also confirms that Lord Nelson was indeed shot from the *Redoubtable* Mizzen top (approximately 15 yards from the part of the deck where Lord Nelson stood). The trajectory of the bullet and the way it broke

4. Published 1 January 1894 as *The War Library* (edited and published by Professor Edward Arber, FSA, etc).

bones on entering the body – and its course thereafter – meant that it could only have originated from aloft. And, if this is indeed the case, what better position than an already dead ship, a good place for a sniper to hide and stalk the ultimate prey?

Beatty continues:

Course and site of the Ball, as ascertained since death.

The ball struck the fore part of his Lordship's epaulette and entered the left shoulder (The famous portrait *The Death of Nelson* by A W Devis, 1807, shows his right shoulder bandaged rather than his left.) immediately before the processus acromion scapulae, which it slightly fractured. It then descended obliquely into the thorax, fracturing the second and third ribs, and after penetrating the left lobe of the lungs, and dividing in its passage a large branch of the pulmonary artery, it entered the left side of the spine between the sixth and seventh dorsal vertebrae, fractured the left transverse process of the sixth dorsal vertebra, wounded the medulla spinalis and, fracturing the right transverse process of the seventh vertebra, made its way from the right side of the spine, directing its course through the muscles of the back, and lodged therein, about 2 inches below the interior angle of the right scapula. On removing the ball, a portion of the gold lace and pad of the epaulette, together with a small piece of his Lordship's coat, was found firmly attached to it.

For Lord Nelson to be shot from deck level, he would have had to be bent double. Also, another minor point for the sceptics and conspiracy theorists to note: the *Redoubtable* had been firmly taken; the only men left alive were up in the Mizzen. Logically, the shot had to have originated from there.

But this presents another – very interesting – theory: Was the sniper already wounded when he delivered the killer shot? As the ship had been taken, it's quite probable that he was, although it can't be proved. But, even so, how good was the shot that killed Lord Nelson?

Well, actually, it was terrible. When we look at the accuracy of a shot fired from the Mizzen top to the quarter deck by a Trafalgar musket, distance, cross-wind, gunsmoke and ship movement are only a few of the obstacles that must be overcome. The job will be even more difficult if the sniper is injured.

Here's another passage from Beatty's book:

It is by no means certain, though highly probable, that Lord Nelson was particularly aimed at by the Enemy. There were only two Frenchmen left alive in the Mizzen top of the *Redoubtable* at the time of his Lordship being wounded, and by the hands of one of these he fell. These men continued firing at captains Hardy and Adair, Lieutenant Rotely of the Marines, and some of the midshipmen on the *Victory*'s poop, for some time afterwards. At length one of them was killed by a musket ball, and on the other's then attempting to escape from the top down the rigging, Mr Pollard (midshipman) fired his musket at him, and shot him in the back, when he fell dead from the shrouds, on the *Redoubtable* poop.

There is much evidence in the above piece – not just an eyewitness account of the death of the sniper who killed Lord Nelson (whichever one of the two shooters on the Mizzen he was) but also the telling line 'These men kept firing at captains Hardy and Adair…'

The snipers were taking pot-shots, and that is no sniper action, even for 1805. The very fact that they shot at two other important captains – and constantly missed – indicates that either they weren't exactly the cream of the marksman crop or that they were injured. Obviously, they picked Lord Nelson out in the crowd – and, as the gunsmoke cleared, a one-armed officer covered in decorations was a prime target – but how many bullets went astray, possibly killing other sailors aboard HMS *Victory*, before Lord Nelson was hit?

What interests us deeply about sniping is not just the accuracy of any famous shot but also its complexity. How uncomfortable was the sniper during a great kill? Did he get away with it? Was he wholly successful with his first shot, as surely he had to be? Actually, in the thick of battle, this last point need not necessarily be true; his incompetence could be covered by the chaos that ensued around him – and, in the case of Lord Nelson's death, we are convinced that that was indeed the case. The two snipers located an area of the deck thick with officers. They located Lord Nelson and started shooting at him. Did they know which one of them killed him? Yes, of course, they did. (As we discuss in the next chapter, a sniper must look the enemy in the eye and the shot isn't completed until the target is reached). And it cost both men dear; HMS *Victory*'s men started firing back and they were killed.

But who gets the credit for killing Lord Nelson's sniper? For many years, the definitive study of Lord Nelson was Robert Southey's *The Life Of Nelson* (published in 1813). Southey took a conservative approach by crediting both John Pollard and Midshipman Francis Edward Collingwood for avenging Nelson's assassin. Beatty's report seems to be a fair reflection of this, because nobody knows which of the two snipers shot Lord Nelson.

Interestingly, on 13 May 1863, a letter appeared in *The Times* from John Pollard, who wrote:

It is true my old shipmate Collingwood who has now been dead some years came up on the poop for a short time. I had discovered the men crouching in the top of *Redoubtable* and pointed them out to him, when he took up his musket and fired once; he then left the poop, I conclude, to return to his station on the quarter-deck... I remained firing till there was not a man to be seen in the top; the last one I saw coming down the Mizzen rigging and he fell from my fire also... I was ushered into the ward room, where Sir Thomas Hardy and other officers were assembled and complimented by them as the person who avenged Lord Nelson's death.

For us, the aging Pollard here displays a little too much self-glorification and Collingwood is deliberately discredited (when he has no opportunity of return comment). However, we do believe that there are a few nuggets of quality information in the letter. For example, Pollard noticed the snipers 'crouching in the top'. They hadn't been noticed before and somebody had to have spotted them – maybe after that fatal shot? If Pollard was the one who spotted the snipers and killed one of them, perhaps he believed that the glory and honour of such an act should go to him? Especially if Collingwood walked off after 'one shot'.

However, Beatty's account, in conjunction with Southey's conservative approach, suggests that Collingwood killed one of the snipers. So, do we believe he did it in one shot, as suggested by Pollard? Surely, if that was the case, Collingwood was the most professional sniper at the Battle of Trafalgar, making a kill and walking away without injury, whereas Lord Nelson's assassin(s) were both killed after giving away their position and taking pot-shots.

So, 200 years after the Battle of Trafalgar, we can confirm that

Lord Nelson was killed by a French sniper – either not a very good one or an injured one – from the Mizzen top of the *Redoubtable*, but we conclude that the best shooter/sniper on the day was quite possibly Midshipman Collingwood. And, as for Pollard taking the credit, his letter casts doubts in the minds of Trafalgar academics, albeit for understandable reasons, but clearly Collingwood's victim must have been Nelson's true sniper. Collingwood picked out the man who had positioned himself in the most tight and secure (although exposed) position, but that was the man who had been making the most accurate shot(s), even though possibly wounded himself.

As for the praise bestowed upon Pollard, if it was deserved – and, believe it or not, we *do* believe the praise was given and was indicative of a superior officer's perception within the Royal Navy at that time – it was a general praise to all able-bodied seamen in the fleet, intended to raise morale after the death of their greatest strategist, motivator and leader. It is well documented that the heads of the ordinary sailors dropped on hearing of the death of Lord Nelson. Morale had to be restored.

Although Lord Nelson died at the Battle of Trafalgar, his efforts won it for the English fleet. Eighteen of the thirty-five enemy vessels were destroyed and more than 4,400 sailors from the combined French and Spanish fleets were killed. Nelson lost 449 men – including himself – but no ships.

The legacy of the Battle of Trafalgar is enormous. To begin with, it ended any chance of Napoleon gaining control of the English Channel and invading Britain. In fact, Napoleon was land-based from then on, concluding with his defeat at the hands of the Duke of Wellington at Waterloo.

Trafalgar also ensured British control of the world's oceans for more than a century after the battle, which simply highlights the importance of the battle and the magnitude of Lord Nelson's great strategy, The Nelson Touch.

But what about the sniper that killed Lord Nelson? In reality, we don't know which man in the Mizzen top fired the shot. And, perhaps as importantly – at least, for a student of sniping – we don't know if the assassin was physically injured when shooting Lord Nelson or whether he was simply a bad, but lucky, shot. What we do know is that the shot *was* executed eventually, and that the unknown sniper was certainly killed by return fire.

The manner of Nelson's death sent shock waves through the hearts of every military officer in the field, regardless of their importance. They were all reminded that they were mortal, and, whether the shot was skilled or lucky, it was, after all, the shot that counted and went down in history. So, by default, the lucky pot-shot becomes an important sniper shot because of the legacy it leaves. Lord Nelson was a celebrity and, like that of John Lennon nearly 200 years later, the manner of his death affected every other celebrity of his day.

Yes, the sniper had arrived, but the true sniper at Trafalgar was Collingwood – one man with one bullet – not a lucky Frenchman.

To conclude this chapter, we would like to clarify another often incorrectly related story concerning the death of Lord Nelson.

Most people believe that his Lordship's last words were 'Kiss me, Hardy' and that, after Captain Hardy had carried out the request, Lord Nelson died.

This, however, isn't the truth of the matter – and we're ignoring the theory that Lord Nelson could have said 'Kismet, Hardy', because of the words uttered by his Lordship directly afterwards: 'Now I am satisfied. Thank God I have done my duty.' At this point, Hardy stood over Nelson in silence for a moment or two, then knelt again and kissed the Lord's forehead again. 'Who is that?' the dying man asked and, on being informed, replied, 'God bless you, Hardy.'

At this point Hardy returned to the upper deck and Lord Nelson requested to be turned on to his side. Nelson then said, 'I wish I had not left the deck, for I shall soon be gone.' But, in the few moments he had left, he said to Chaplain Scott, 'Doctor, I have *not* been a *great* sinner.' There was a short pause. Then: 'Remember that I leave Lady Hamilton and my daughter Horatia as a legacy to my country.' His words became difficult to discern then, but he was then heard to say, 'Thank God I have done my duty.' These words he repeated and, according to many books and features concerning Lord Nelson, they were officially his last words.

Again, however, this is wrong. As Southey correctly related in his biography *The Life of Nelson*, Chaplain Scott – obviously a highly respected member of the crew – saw that his Lordship was attempting to speak moments before he fell into a death coma. He bent closely over Lord Nelson and faintly heard the murmured words, 'God and my country.' It would appear that Lord Nelson was saying a prayer; indeed, he wrote one shortly before the battle took place, and the words 'God' and 'my country' are grouped very close together at the start of that prayer. A delirious Lord Nelson therefore could only manage 'God and my country' from his own Trafalgar prayer – fitting last words for a man who held both in such a proud place within his heart.

> May the Great God, whom I worship,
> grant to my Country, and for the benefit
> of Europe in general, a great and
> glorious Victory; and
> may no misconduct, in anyone,
> tarnish it; and may humanity after

victory be the predominant feature in
the British Fleet.
For myself individually, I commit
my life to Him who made me and
may His blessing light upon my
endeavours for serving my Country
faithfully.

To Him I resign myself and the just
cause which is entrusted to me to
defend.

AMEN, AMEN, AMEN

NELSON'S PRAYER, WRITTEN WITH THE ENEMY IN SIGHT,
SHORTLY BEFORE THE BATTLE OF TRAFALGAR

Lord Nelson, as we are told by popular history, died at 1630hrs
once he heard that the Battle of Trafalgar had been won.
Observing Beatty's words, Nelson either died at 1515hrs, or
1600hrs (he mentions that Nelson lasted two hours and then two
hours forty-five minutes in *Death of Lord Nelson*). If either is true
– and we cannot dispute it because he was there and we weren't –
then Lord Nelson never heard that victory was his, that was
simply a piece of propaganda to keep morale in the ranks and, let's
face it, that was fully justified.

CHAPTER FOUR

Snipers of the Great War

'Sir Douglas Haig's Chief of Staff [visited] the Passchendaele
front... When he saw the mud and ghastly conditions under
which the soldiers had fought and died, he was horrified and
said... "Why was I never told about this before?"'
THE MEMOIRS OF FIELD-MARSHAL MONTGOMERY

Too many people died senselessly during the Great War.
The term 'great' evokes thoughts of immense suffering, a
furtherance of the evil that the human race can bestow upon itself.
Incredible technology was harnessed during its modest four-year
span, between the years 1914 and 1918, resulting in a crushingly
heavy death toll.

A bizarre – almost macabre – juxtaposition occurred as old
techniques blurred with the new. Cavalrymen charged into battle
on horseback wearing gas masks, only to be blown away by rifle
and bomb. The old was overtaken by the new, and the tacticians
weren't ready for it. Consequently, many mistakes were made and
so many lives were taken.

The evil of the Great War didn't end at the eleventh hour of the eleventh day of the eleventh month; so much spilled over into the Second World War approximately twenty-five years later. The evil of the Nazis' Final Solution would sicken the whole of mankind forever afterwards, but even that had its roots in the Great War.

It's not the mission of this chapter to detail the mutation of the German Empire between the First and Second World Wars, but it's worth mentioning the sudden impact that the Great War had on all war scenarios that followed it. The battles, the waste, the suffering was much more intense, and out of that hell emerged a specially trained soldier: a sniper. Not just the odd one, but a strategic number.

The stories already told so far in this book concern sniper activity, but here we're putting a stake in the ground with the Great War as the birth of the contemporary sniper – i.e. the sniper as we view him today.

This chapter looks at the sniper of the Great War, his tactics, his weapons, his strategy and his way of life – a way of life far removed from the military sniper of today, or indeed the Second World War, as we will see in later chapters. The sniper of the Great War was the raw bones on which the military would soon add flesh and create a sophisticated killing machine.

Does all that sound exciting? Impressive? Or even just plain interesting? Maybe. But before we get carried away in our analysis of our Great War sniper, let's look at the suffering of the victim and, ostensibly, the cowardice of the sniper.

Passchendaele

Rain fell heavily throughout October 1916. The whole area around the desiccated village of Passchendaele had been turned into a 'porridge of mud'. Horses were drowned, sinking in the mud under too heavy loads; sixteen stretcher-bearers were needed instead of the normal two for one solitary stretcher.

That was October. November and December were far worse. In the battlefield, there was a furtherance of the hell of the previous months, as Gough stated, 'Men of the strongest physique could hardly move forward at all and became victims to enemy's snipers.'

Young and fit men would suddenly slip in the mud, then either begin to sink or just stick there, up to their waist. They would then become terrified children awaiting an inevitable fate – a fate that soon came. As a friend's head exploded in a shower of blood and bone, the men would start to scream, the skin blood and raw flesh of the dead – their friends and colleagues – drenching them until they in turn were murdered.

What a catch! These men were good target practice for enemy snipers. And many more would meet a similar fate.

This barbarism was prevalent during the Second World War, especially where the commandant of one concentration camp gave his son half a dozen Jews with which to practise his sniper skills as a birthday present.

Does all this sound too over-the-top? If so, please take note of the following passage from Field-Marshal Montgomery's memoirs, where, as a humble Lieutenant during the Great War, he nearly fell foul of a German sniper himself: 'I [was] shot through the chest... I had fallen in the open ... A soldier ran to me and began to put a field dressing on my wound; he was shot through the head by a sniper and collapsed on top of me. The sniper continued to fire at us and I got a second wound in the knee; the soldier received many bullets intended for me.'

The snipers of the Great War were keen and brutal, but what did they have to endure for their art?

The Great War Sniper

The snipers of the Great War were architects and strategists, not unlike their future counterparts. They would dig pits on the edge of No Man's Land just long enough and deep enough for them to slip into and take comfortable aim. Although these holes gave a little shelter from the elements, the rain would set their sides crumbling into slimy water. Already damp, cold and cramped, the sniper would wait until the last moment to escape back to his section. Such are the ways of the lone gunman.

Abandoned buildings provided a great vantage point for the sniper during the Great War. More often than not, these had the advantage of being away from the muck and bullets, giving the sniper a position from which he could pick off the enemy – like those poor fellows stuck in the mud. But to be in a relatively secure and comfortable position wasn't really the norm for the sniper of the Great War.

Now, let's not confuse the soldier with the sniper. The sniper never pursues; that was never his job. Instead, he lies in wait and picks off his victim calmly, methodically. At the Battle of Trafalgar, Midshipman Collingwood took a calm shot amidst the surrounding carnage – one man, one bullet.

During the First World War, some snipers would lie for hours on their belly in No Man's Land, waiting for a head to pop up above a trench. Then *blam!* a bullet in the skull. *But there's been no fire for hours. Where the hell did that come from?* Then *blam!* – a mug of tea in the face of a friend as the second victim takes a bullet in the forehead for being inquisitive.

Any more for any more? Anger overspills. Three men jump over the top, firing blindly into No Man's Land. *Blam! Blam! Blam!* Three dead bodies sinking into the mud in the pissing rain.

Sniper Image

As with the technique of sniping, the image of the sniper was also forged during the Great War.

Yes the sniper was feared and revered, but he was hated and

called a coward, too. Why shoot from the shadows? *Come out and fight like a real man!*

But that's not the sniper's way. He sees a target. He hits it. He then waits for the second target.

The sniper earned his reputation for stealth and effectiveness during the Great War and expanded upon it during the Second World War, especially in battles like that of Stalingrad, which will be examined in detail later. Again, though, the concept of sniping was a new one; the trained military sniper would become an awesome foe, killing and maiming before the soldier – or the officer – became educated as to the sniper's terrible power.

And it was this terrible power that was the most important quality, for the sniper knew where the mud was thickest, he knew where the high ground was, he knew where the best ground vantage point was and what escape routes to take. His terrible power lay in understanding the terrain and, most specifically, in being able to find his way in the dark. He was tenacious and dangerous, a character who never played by the rules. He would camouflage himself and wait for the enemy to show himself. Then the enemy would die – and they wouldn't even know where the bullets had come from.

So the sniper was viewed as the vermin of soldiering and not the total professional who had a personal standard of excellence over the infantryman. He kept a careful log – a diary of kills that, in no time at all, could climb into the hundreds. He was a strange beast, but he nevertheless demanded respect.

But who had the better snipers during the Great War: the British or the Germans? To answer this question, we must first look at the rifles used by both sets of snipers.

Weaponry
The German Sniper Rifle

During the Great War, the Germans exclusively used variations of the Mauser Rifle (1898–1914). At the turn of the century, German troops were using c/98 and c/02 – the first Mauser rifles to be granted patents, in 1898 and 1902 respectively. Both rifles were trialled with the German infantry but both failed to impress, the latter because it was too cumbersome.

The rifles that did impress, however, were c/06/08 and that Aviator's rifle, model 16. Taking the c/06/08 first, this rifle had three short-recoil designs with different locking systems. The first used a flap system similar to the Friberg-Kjellman system, comprising two rear-pivoted locking flaps supporting the rear of the bolt that were moved in and out of recesses in the receiver by barrel recoil. Two variants of this system discarded the flaps and substituted a block in the form of a saddle, whereby the breech-block slid back in this saddle, which was cammed in and out of a recess in the top of the receiver. Tests of this design continued until the outbreak of war in 1914 without the army coming to any decision over which weapon to use, so it became, almost by default, the first German military sniper rifle.

The Aviator's rifle, model 16, became the dominant German rifle during the Great War, although they were made primarily for use with balloon crews, before the arrival of the flexible machine gun. Once machine guns could be produced in sufficient numbers for the aviation service, the Aviator rifle was abandoned, although some managed to appear on the Western Front as infantry sniper weapons. By this time, however, they had managed to collect full-length stocks and bayonets. The model 16 had its origin in the flap-locking version of the c/06/08.

A third weapon – the 1916 Mauser rifle – required oiled cartridges for reliable operation, and suffered from another shortcoming due to the contemporary state of metallurgy, which ensured that the Mausers were all heavy weapons relying on the interaction of cam surfaces and various bearings, all of which wore rapidly. (It's interesting to note that some of the rifle's operating systems were to appear years later, and some of these proved to be quite successful, thanks to the application of better technology.)

The British Sniper Rifle

Where the Germans had Mauser, the British had Lee-Enfield. When the short-magazine Lee-Enfield was introduced into service, it met with heavy criticism. As the November 1908 edition of *Arms And Explosives* magazine reported, 'The rifle was always bad, its defects always notorious... and the propagation of badness will doubtless continue for several more generations to come.' Maybe because of this heavy criticism, the UK's War Office developed a rifle more in line with what the critics wanted. Interestingly, the result was based on the Mauser bolt action and was .276-inch (7mm) calibre.

After extensive experimentation, both in theory and practice, the short-magazine Lee-Enfield was approved for issue on a trial basis as the 'Rifle Magazine, .276in Pattern 1914' in 1913. The cartridge it used was roughly based on the .280-inch Ross model and was exceptionally powerful. Loaded with cordite, the results included excessive muzzle flash and blast, severe erosive wear, barrel overheating, irregular chamber pressures and premature ignition due to the heat of the barrel. Before these problems could be solved, however, the outbreak of war caused the entire project to be shelved indefinitely.

In late 1914, the problems of mass producing the Lee-Enfield rifle led to the design being reassessed. The rifle had been designed with an eye to mass production, so it was rapidly converted to the standard .303 calibre and manufacturing contracts were placed in the USA. The rifles were eventually brought into British service on 21 June 1916 as the 'Pattern 1914' or 'P 14'.

The short-magazine Lee-Enfield rifle can be recognised by the long exposed muzzle and prominent wings protecting the foresight, by the distinctive shape of the rear sight housing and by the fact that there is no exposed magazine. Although the weapon had been designed to the satisfaction of the target fraternity, it wasn't liked by the soldiers. The P 14 was too long, poorly balanced and cumbersome in combat, especially when fitted with a long bayonet. The number of such rifles issued during the Great War is not known, but most of them turned up during the Second World War as the typical weapon of the Home Guard.

So, during the Great War, the British didn't really have a good weapon; they had an American version of a British weapon that was in development. The Germans, on the other hand, had something all of their own but that was also poorly designed.

So what does all this tell us about the Great War snipers? Primarily that they were forging the basis of the modern sniper in the most bloody and terrible way. Those that survived learned a lot, and that experience would provide the snipers of the Second World War with more professionalism in both weapon technology and sniper technique.

The Great War was one of mankind's most horrific and gruesome activities of the twentieth century, and – typically – the human race learned much from the experience, as far as technology and military professionalism was concerned. While it's regrettable that such immense developments can be made only through conflict, that does seem to be the trend throughout history. The human race learns – slowly – through its mistakes. Unfortunately, it makes such mistakes again and again.

CHAPTER FIVE

All Quiet on the Western Front

> 'It could easily have happened that we wouldn't be
> sitting on our boxes here today, it was all so damned close.
> And because of that, everything is new and full of life –
> the red poppies, the good food, the cigarettes and the
> summer breeze.'
>
> ENRICH MARIA REMARQUE, ALL QUIET ON THE WESTERN FRONT

When we were checking through this book, it became apparent to us that, by the end of the previous chapter, there was a natural respect emerging for the sniper. We therefore decided to insert a 'bridge' chapter that showcased two major points: the suffering of the human being (especially that of the enemy) during times of war, and the contemporary perception of the sniper in the early twentieth century.

The easiest way to tackle these two important but subtle points was to write a chapter concerning *Im Westen Nichts Neues* – or, as English readers know it, *All Quiet On The Western Front* – a harrowing novel concerning the Great War written by the German author Erich Maria Remarque.

Even in its English translation, Remarque's 1929 novel is a powerful work that speaks from the ranks, discussing the senseless waste of human life from the *enemy*'s point of view. And the irony is that the enemy was the one making the harrowing observations. He was saying that it was all a terrible waste, he was saying that he was going through hell, he was saying that his good friends were being killed horribly by *his* enemy.

Here's one scene from Remarque's novel: 'Josef Behm, a tubby, cheerful chap... Oddly enough [he] was one of the first killed. He was shot in the eye during an attack, and we left him for dead.'

There's so much to analyse within this passage. Firstly, the narrator's 'cheerful' friend is murdered by Tommy. Now, that's a turnaround to begin with. Surely Tommy wouldn't kill a cheerful, God-fearing man, and especially so disgustingly? But yes, he did. And the reputed good guy is suddenly as bad as the bad guy. Secondly, Behm is 'shot in the eye', implying a single surprise shot. This is sniper activity, surely? But the word 'sniper' (or sharpshooter, or lone gunman; let's just call him sniper for this argument) isn't used in the novel, and for a work of 1929 this does give rise to an extremely important point, and something scholars have been messing up for years: coherent supposition.

As will be discussed in the next chapter, we know that the British, especially, were training snipers for the Great War, but the important thing to observe is that, in hindsight, while the genesis and path of the sniper might be very clear from the start of the twentieth century to the present day, in reality the path isn't so clear. The ordinary soldier wouldn't differentiate between a 'sniper' and any other infantryman, especially through the Great War and up to the Second World War.

Observe the follow-up quote from the passage quoted above: 'That afternoon we suddenly heard him shout out and saw him crawling around in no man's land... Because he couldn't see and was mad with pain he didn't take cover, so he was shot down from the other side before anyone could get out and fetch him.'

Again, this is classic sniper action – a single man being taken out by a single shot (at least, that's what is implied) – but again the word 'sniper' isn't used, which reinforces the point that the word wasn't in common usage. Even so, the tactics of the sniper *were* in common use, and they're peppered throughout *All Quiet On The Western Front*, from throwaway lines such as 'We see men go on living with the top of their skulls missing' – due to mortar or sniper action? The concept of the sniper doesn't even enter the narrator's mind.

Here's another interesting line: 'Modern trench warfare demands knowledge and experience; you have to have a good grasp of the lie of the land, have the sounds and effects of the different shells in your ears.' This piece is very important because, while it illustrates the narrator's awareness of enemy snipers, it indicates that this awareness concerns only heavy artillery attack!

So again, where is the sniper? In fact, *All Quiet On The Western Front* doesn't need snipers to be so terribly harrowing; it works on hope, fear, anger, despair and, finally, submission, and that hasn't really changed in any war.

There is a danger with writing from the viewpoint of hindsight, clearly logging the history of a sniper back to his natural conception. Reading 'contemporary' accounts or worse – for instance, personal reminiscences that use the word 'sniper', thus placing it into the context of common usage of the early twentieth century – gives a false impression of the development of the sniper. The sniper was not a common beast in the early twentieth century; he was a child growing and about to take his exams.

Yes, he was an evolving beast, a beast in motion, gathering skills and, yes, having great success, but, as *All Quiet On The Western Front* makes clear, he wasn't classified as something separate from the common enemy, as a highly dangerous solitary entity; that would only really happen during the Second World War. This is a very important point because the fact that the sniper was somewhat unappreciated explains why he was so successful and why strategists made so many tactical errors in battle scenarios during the Great War.

So much for the great sniper of the Great War. Now let's take a look at the horrors of the Great War, described so harrowingly but brilliantly in *All Quiet On The Western Front*. This chapter doesn't exist simply to explain the unappreciated stance of the sniper during the Great War but to serve as a wake-up call for any sniper student reading this book and thinking that it all sounds like jolly good fun. We're talking about taking lives here, about killing an 'enemy', sometimes slowly. The snipers of the Western armed forces are highly trained professionals who have a duty to their country. Theirs isn't an easy job, and it has its ghosts. This chapter is intended as a watchword to the young: there is no glamour in sniping; it is a job for the highly trained elite in extreme circumstances.

We don't get a moment's sleep during the night. Seven men die in our room. One of them sings snatches of hymns in a high, strained tenor for an hour until it gives way to the death rattle. Another gets out of bed and crawls to the window… He wanted to look out for the last time.

ERICH MARIA REMARQUE, ALL QUIET ON THE WESTERN FRONT

All Quiet On The Western Front has been the Achilles heel of the politician – and, indeed, the soldier – as it attests in no uncertain terms that war was a dreadful thing replete with shades of grey, not an enemy that wore black and killed without remorse or reason. But maybe that's the great contradiction of the novel; maybe that's why the sniper isn't identified within the covers of the book – because he does kill without rhyme or reason.

Hours. The gurgling starts up again – how long it takes for a man to die! What I do know is that he is beyond saving... If I hadn't lost my revolver when I was crawling along, I would shoot him. I can't stab him... This is the first man I have ever killed with my own hands, the first one I've seen at close quarters whose death I've caused.

Erich Maria Remarque, All Quiet On The Western Front

CHAPTER SIX

Vasily Zaitsev –
An Animal Instinct

'Zaitsev is so different from Stalingrad that the city masks him,
even protects him, the way snow covers the spring tulip bulbs;
because in some way, some intuitive hunter's way of being *in* but
not actually *of* the forest, the city cannot even touch him.'
DAVID L ROBBINS, *WAR OF THE RATS*

Through his exploits depicted on celluloid and in the
pages of David L Robbins's grimly exciting Second World
War novel *War Of The Rats*, Vasily Zaitsev has become a legend
in the world of snipers. While discussing his character with both
historians and fellow shooters, however, we've always been
presented with two diametrically opposed views: that Zaitsev was
either a hero of Mother Russia or a clever publicity stunt created
to motivate a nation that was being crushed by the ruthless
German war machine. [6]

For the purposes of this chapter, we'll assume that Zaitsev was the most famous sniper of all time, with the possible exception of Lee Harvey Oswald [*sic*]. However, in order to play Devil's advocate for a few moments, we should consider if there could be any truth to the extraordinary claim that Zaitsev's exploits could have been massively exaggerated.

During the writing of this book, we were fortunate enough to acquire an English translation of some elements of a KGB 'handbook'. The ultimate aim of this publication was a little unclear, as were the origins of the 'Top Secret' instructions contained therein (as current and ex-government officers, neither of us can even imagine where the publishers sourced this data), but there were unquestionably some fascinating and enlightening chapters that were verifiable. One in particular concentrated on the extreme levels of deception and suppression employed by the Stalin regime. Within this chapter were some 'official' photographs doctored by the KGB under Stalin's orders. One original photograph showed Stalin flanked by around seven very senior military officers, all of whom held prominent positions in his government. The same photograph was then shown again, reissued after a few years, but with Stalin flanked by only a few of the original officers. It was without doubt the same source photograph: the background was unchanged and Stalin's pose and uniform were identical, as were those of his remaining comrades. However, through what was to become a deadly form of natural wastage, some of the staff in the original photograph fell out of favour with their masters and had their very existence extinguished, as well as their lives.

6. It is an accepted fact by the writers of this book and novelist David L Robbins (see his standalone interview later in the book) that Zaitsev was a real person. However, because there is a school of thought that holds that he was a 'publicity stunt', this perception must be addressed in this chapter. Robbins gives further insight during his interview.

Stalin had these unfortunate characters erased from the photograph.

If a government is capable of such deception, is it not also conceivable that the exploits of a super-sniper, who was to become a beacon of hope to the embattled people of Stalingrad, were exaggerated or, indeed, fabricated from scratch? The answer is, of course, yes, but, in order to make anything we say in this chapter meaningful, we must assure people that Zaitsev was real.

As we look more closely at Zaitsev's achievements and the conditions in which he fought, we should perhaps take his phenomenally high number of kills with a little pinch of gunpowder.

Vasily Zaitsev was born near the cold mountains of the Urals. From the age of four, he was taught the skills required by the hunter, which many of us who have an appreciation for the outdoors still cherish and pass on to our own children. Stealth and infinite patience are the fundamentals of stalking prey, but the real skill – the ability to methodically track prey to the point at which you can secretly watch it through a sniper scope – is developed from an early age. The ability to blend into nature, to embrace it and therefore to be at one with your surroundings, is a key tactic of the successful sniper. Although these skills can be taught in later life to deadly effect, we genuinely believe that the natural hunter and stalker will always have the edge on the soldier pulled from the infantry ranks because he's a good shot.

As a child hunter and stalker, Zaitsev would have been taught skills that take years to perfect and understand in military training. He learned his skills in the field, however, and over a much longer time than any military sniper recruit. (Ensuring that you're downwind of your prey is technically of no benefit when resting your crosshairs on a weary German soldier in the ruins of Stalingrad, for instance, yet such an inherent ability, which would have come naturally to Zaitsev, contributed to his being someone who was more than a textbook sharpshooter.)

Zaitsev naturally took extraordinary instinctive measures to be hidden from the view of both the prey and other members of the pack. His natural instinct was basic, animal-like and hungry.

We believe that Zaitsev and his fellow Red snipers – some of whom will be mentioned later in this chapter – epitomise the ethos of the sniper. Hunting animals is a bloody business, as the kill is more often than not retrieved and butchered. Often the sniper's shot is perceived as a surgical cut – the keyhole surgery of the battlefield – but this is not truly the case. The sniper's shot is brutal, both to the shooter and to the target. A sniper must be prepared to look his prey in the eye, to see him blink, smile, yawn. To see him talking to a colleague. To see him sigh as the battlefield takes its toll on his morale. The humanity of the sniper's target, his very essence of life, is far more apparent to the sharpshooter than to the foot soldier who shoots multiple targets at 200m, or to the artillery officer who kills arbitrarily at 8km. The sniper must witness the target shatter as the high-velocity rifle bullet pierces his skull and removes the back of his head. As a seasoned hunter, Zaitsev would have been under no illusions about the damage he was causing, and this coldness would have been essential when he used the scope to select a victim.

The first time you use a rifle with a scope, it is indeed quite a shock to see how close the target appears. When pointing the weapon at a paper target, this is a real benefit, but one can only imagine how difficult it must be when the face of the intended victim seems only a few feet away. It is tantamount to walking up to someone and firing a handgun at point-blank range between their eyes.

As well as the psychological trauma of sniping, the shooters of Stalingrad fought in one of the most hostile environments known to man: the urban battlefield. The geographic scale of urban conflict is much smaller than that of fighting in open ground. For the foot soldier, the enemy can be only feet away, and for the sniper the range might be as little as 300m. This was recently and very vividly illustrated when the US Army moved into Falluja in November 2004. As the last of the Iraqi insurgency collapsed, we saw live in our living rooms haunting images of terrified troops in squads of six men walking in a huddled group through old, overhanging Middle Eastern streets, each man desperately trying to cover all possible angles: left, right, up, down.

Combine this fighting environment with biting-cold temperatures and the skill of the sniper is put to the ultimate test. Not only does he have to understand the ballistics of a bullet in cold air but he also has to maintain the patience required to wait hidden for the right kill in sub-zero temperatures while exposed to the increased danger of urban warfare.

Stalingrad epitomised the worst aspects of the urban battlefield. From August 1942 to February 1943, the city was systematically destroyed as invading German forces and Russian defenders clashed at this strategic crossing point of the Volga River. The battle for Stalingrad ultimately proved to be a fatal blow to the proud German Army. While Hitler had already failed in his plans to attack other major Russian cities, the fact that this particular city was named after his nemesis made it an irresistible target. Against the advice of his generals, Hitler ordered his troops to surround the city, trapping thousands of Russian civilians and soldiers within its boundaries. As part of what was to be known as Operation Barbarossa, Hitler was single-mindedly determined that Stalingrad should fall, firmly believing not only that the collapse of the city would lead to the capture of valuable oil fields and territory but also that the fall of Stalingrad would mark the end of Russia itself.

The German offensive on Stalingrad began on 23 August 1942, and it was brutal. Luftwaffe aircraft carried out intense bombing raids on all parts of the city and German tracked artillery began to occupy the perimeter. From all sides and above, the occupants of Stalingrad were subjected to a storm of high explosives and incoming fire. Before long, this onslaught created a landscape littered with only the skeletons of buildings, a nightmarish battleground that would see some of the bloodiest hand-to-hand combat of the Second World War. Pockets of the city fell into German hands and were retaken, only to fall again. Streets and even single rooms within buildings became frontlines. Tales abounded of German and Russian troops fighting with short-range firearms and bastardisations of medieval bladed weapons just to claim a single house. In a war that had seen the emergence of sophisticated firearms and explosives, one can only imagine the fighting conditions that once again spawned the use of clubs inset with nails.

It was into this world, as part of the 284th Division, that Vasily Zaitsev began his personal war against the German invaders.

To the sniper, the urban environment is both a blessing and a curse. It provides innumerable places to hide and limitless shadows in which to conceal yourself, but equally you're often very vulnerable to return fire and escape routes are not always readily available.

Take, for example, the traditional sniper haunt of a very high position giving a commanding view of a city square. This position is seemingly ideal to take out a soldier on point duty as his squad enters the kill zone. Ranging is easy as the firing position is probably only 200–300m away from the lead target. Or the sniper can choose to wait for a few moments, until the entire squad is in view and he can assess who is the senior officer. Shoot the top-ranking man and you immediately throw the squad into chaos as the number two tries to take control of a unit of men too afraid to emerge from behind their hastily acquired cover.

This scene was given above-average Hollywood treatment in a film that portrayed a band of US soldiers in D-Day France attempting to save a private named Ryan. Credit should be given to the director, Steven Spielberg, who even illustrated the harsh tactic of the sniper leaving the first target alive in the hope that a fellow trooper will expose himself in an effort to render vital first aid. (It's worth pointing out, however, that this is a very dangerous tactic for the sniper, as he is clearly intending to fire a second shot rather than 'shoot and scoot'. As discussed in chapter one, staying in place effectively halves your chances of not being spotted.)

Two of the most famous sniper photographs of all time grimly show this sniping manoeuvre in a similar scenario during some of the worst fighting in the Vietnam War. The first hazy black-and-white photograph shows a badly wounded US Marine lying on his back on a slight incline. The terrain is dry and dusty with very low brush. There are large patches of clear ground, and the Marine is lying in one of them. There is no obvious near cover or concealment. The man has lost his helmet and his M14 weapon is out of reach, but he is very much alive. Clearly, he has been badly wounded by incoming fire. He could have been hit by a piece of shrapnel, but we know from the account of his fellow soldiers that he was selected and hit by an unseen Viet Cong sniper. Advancing towards him, with his back to the photographer, is another Marine in a low crouch. The second soldier has no weapon but wears a Red Cross armband and a medical kit on his back. The tension in the photograph is palpable.

The next photograph, taken only moments later, shows both soldiers lying on the ground together. The wounded Marine looks desperate; the medic is unconscious or dead. The sniper, who had already established an exact range on the first target, had remained in position, knowing that a medic would be sent for. What would you do next? Send another medic? Until you have a fix on the sniper's position, you can't even call for immediate air or artillery support. It's a classic case of a sniper – who may now have taken the chance to flee – holding back an entire unit of highly trained men armed with automatic weapons.

Looking back to the D-Day urban scenario with a sniper in a high position – perhaps a tower or church spire – one can argue that this will give him a textbook kill zone. In reality, however, this firing point will leave him very vulnerable to detection. It's logical to assume that the commander of the unit under attack will initially direct all his available firepower at obvious sniper positions, and there's also a good chance that someone will have seen the rifle flash or smoke. This situation is also demonstrated in *Saving Private Ryan*, where the US sniper who eventually kills the German sniper is himself killed in a church tower by German artillery. The restrictive high position is a deathtrap. The main reason why this position can become so dangerous is because it prevents the shooter from observing the first fundamental rule of sniping, especially in urban combat. It's a rule that Vasily Zaitsev knew very well: shoot and move.

A sniper must have an immediate escape route. Muzzle flash from a gun can give away his position, and those attuned to the sound of gunfire can invariably tell where a shot has come from. A sniper must be totally concealed but he must have a back door. In Vasily Zaitsev's fighting ground, it was essential to his survival that he perfected this rule.

Concealment and cover were theoretically abundant in Stalingrad, but before we analyse events further we should take a moment – as Zaitsev would have – to make sure we fully understand both those terms. Chuck Taylor, an eminent US Army colonel and close-range combat expert, gives the following definitions: cover is to hide behind an object which will block incoming fire, while concealment is to be hidden from view, but not necessarily in a position where you're protected from incoming fire. Good examples of cover would therefore be a solid wall and the front end of a car, behind the engine block. Examples of concealment might also be cover, but they could also be trees or tall grass and therefore, by their very structure, not cover.

To a sniper, both cover and concealment are important, but the latter concealment is probably the key criterion, and a good hunter will have an inherent skill for concealing himself. It's possible for a sniper who has matured in the area of personal concealment to fire from a relatively open position yet remain totally invisible to the enemy.

It must be remembered that the sniper was still a relatively new concept even as late as the Second World War. It was only in the latter stages of the Great War that snipers had any form of recognition, and this attitude was still seen in the US Army's conflicts in Korea and Vietnam, where some senior military staff could see no added value in the sniper. Such a man took too much time to train, and there was great uncertainty about the effectiveness of the lone gunman.

This effectively brings us back full circle to our original observation that Vasily Zaitsev, as a hunter and stalker, was already showing the way for future training with his inherent natural skills. Without knowing it, he was forging a path for snipers to come and writing the textbook on sniping.

Recognising these skills, and the high head-count value this new fighting machine was bringing to the war in Stalingrad, the Russian military asked Zaitsev to form a makeshift sniper school in the ruins of a factory, and it was here that Zaitsev taught the basics of his craft to numerous Russian soldiers. The course was only a few days long, but that was enough to provide basic instruction on advanced rifle handling, scope shooting, ballistic performance, sensible target selection and concealment. More importantly,

Zaitsev had an ability to convey and teach the psychology of sniping. He was able to convince the student soldiers that they were capable of performance greater than the sum of their parts. He was able to demonstrate the much overlooked impact of a well-aimed single shot in a world of sustained fire. Consequently, he turned out killers who could deliver 'one shot, one kill' statistics in significant numbers. Compare this to the typical German tactic of massive amounts of ordnance and huge numbers of men and it's possible to see the attraction of Zaitsev's protégés to the resource-strapped Russians.

Some members of the Stalingrad sniper school became almost as famous as Zaitsev himself. Zaitsev's partner, Kulikov, became an integral part of the legend, as did the elusive 'Zikan', who clocked up a significant number of kills.

Soon not only the tacticians but also the huge political machine behind the Russian military came to recognise the impact of Zaitsev. This hunter from the Urals was destined to become not only one of the world's first super-snipers but also a political tool that could be deployed to demoralise a weakening enemy. Flyers were dropped in Stalingrad and military newspapers talked of Zaitsev's achievements. Inevitably, and quite intentionally, these Russian documents made their way into German hands and were duly translated. Zaitsev is thus probably the best example of a sniper having a great psychological, as well as physical, impact on an enemy.

Unlike a full frontal assault, a sniper can perhaps be compared to that most hideous of weapons: the anti-personnel mine. You don't know he's there. There's no warning of an attack, just a fleeting second of recognition that ushers in death and maiming. In fact, perhaps the sniper is even more disconcerting than the mine, as he can attack in silence. Although we know that Zaitsev didn't use a suppressed weapon, his long-range shots would have been nothing more than muffled thumps to the targets, who would be hearing the noise of battle in other parts of the city.

Let's for a moment cast ourselves back to Stalingrad on a cold November evening in 1943. The light has almost faded. Darkness is creeping in from above, and it's now impossible to see into the buildings around you. The ground temperature is below zero. Your hands are so cold that they've gone numb. Breath is clouding in front of your face. You can see five soldiers from the German Sixth Army huddled together in a bomb crater in a ruined street in a ruined city. It is a foreign place, far removed from everything they know and love at home. The bravado of the invincible German Army is gone. This is Hell on Earth. No longer do they feel that they have the love of the Fuehrer behind them, that he's guiding their every step for the greater glory of the Reich. How can sitting here in the freezing cold surrounded by death possibly be part of the Master Plan? They're poorly equipped without proper cold-weather clothing. Two of them don't even have coats and have instead wrapped rags around their hands and faces to ward off the chill air. They dare not light a fire; that would bring instant death by artillery fire. All around them are the sounds of a city waiting for the next day of carnage.

In the inky blackness, a faint cry carries across the ground. Another wounded soldier of undetermined origin has been left for the dogs of the night. It is now pitch dark. Every few moments a flare shoots into the air, casting an ice-cold, flickering blue light over pockmarked ground. Skeletons of buildings rear out of the darkness, only to retreat as the flare dies. There is an ever-present fear of a sniper attack, but the five men all close their eyes to block out the horrors of the day and try to sleep.

One soldier is particularly cold and uncomfortable. His movement annoys his colleagues as they try to lie still and stay warm, but he is too stiff and sore to lie any longer. He moves carefully to his knees to stretch his aching back.

With a sharp crack, like the sound of a bat hitting a baseball, the soldier's head is snapped back and in the distance there is the barely audible thump of a rifle discharge. His body pitches over and his shattered head hits the ground. He is dead before the echo of the shot has faded to silence. The hot blood steams on the frigid ground, melting a small channel in the snow.

The remaining four soldiers are frozen with fear. No matter what their position on the cold ground, they dare not move. Small wonder, then, that they lie awake all night, terrified, staring at their dead friend, who looks back with unseeing, surprised eyes. Could the certain death of a sniper's crosshairs be on them now?

They squeeze even lower on the freezing ground. A whisper of fear spreads amongst them. What is it? Is Zaitsev out there? A Russian document translated by military intelligence told them that he killed twenty-five men this week. Will it be safe, even in the morning, to move away from this position? What if he's still there, just waiting for one of them to make a move? One shot, one kill – four other soldiers targeted not by a bullet but a psychological warrior.

When the Communist Party began to publish stories of Zaitsev's exploits, their primary aim was to boost the morale of a flagging Russian people and army but, in doing so, they also put seasoned German soldiers in the unenviable position of being too afraid to look out from behind walls and trenches.

While Zaitsev undoubtedly qualifies as a sniper, what of the tool of his trade? We've mentioned his rifle in generic terms many times over the course of this chapter, but what made it one of the most famous sniper rifles of all time? Like all Russian snipers, Zaitsev carried a Mosin Nagant M1891/30 sniper rifle, which differed very little from a standard infantry weapon and was a

1930 upgrade to an original 1891 rifle. Like so many wartime sniper rifles, the 91/30 wasn't really a purpose-built gun but part of an upgrade programme that pulled rifles that boasted above-average accuracy from normal production lines.

This is actually a very common practice and is one explored in more detail in the later technical annexes to this book. The barrels of all guns are unique, which makes it forensically possible to match any spent round to the gun that fired it, as the rifling cuts a unique 'fingerprint' into the bullet. Although no two guns have exactly the same rifling, some are machined – more by luck than judgement – with a barrel that delivers a bullet with optimum spin and velocity. During the Second World War, such guns produced by all sides were pulled aside to become sniper rifles.

The original 1891 rifle had a bolt handle that was set at a 90-degree angle to the right of the gun. During the gun's operation, this handle was turned upwards to take the bolt out of battery, then pulled backwards to eject a spent case and pushed forwards and down to load a new round. However, with the bolt being twisted up and back, this prevented the fitting of a scope on the top of the gun. Therefore, the sniper version of the 91/30 had a revised bolt handle fitted, which began life pointing downwards (like that of a Lee-Enfield) and was required to be pulled out of battery only 90 degrees upwards in line with the side of the gun. (This rifle is analysed in more detail later in this book.)

With the top of the rifle now free from obstruction, the Russians fitted it with either a 3.5x or 4x scope. Couple this with a 7.62mm round and you have an effective long-range weapon, one that has since become well respected and, indeed, has fared better in freezing conditions than its more fragile German counterpart: the Mauser 98K.

It is on the theme of Zaitsev's rifle that we often dwell on one minor element of his story. As keen shooters and small-arms collectors, we, the authors, consider ourselves fortunate to belong to an ever-decreasing group of people who still appreciate the aesthetics of a well-made firearm. When Zaitsev was fighting in Stalingrad, he did so in an era when rifles were a work of art and the polymer revolution ushered in by Glock was almost half a decade away. The Nagant, however, was of an old design and was made invariably with poor-quality wood and metal. There was a rugged functionality to the gun, but the Russians were decades away from embracing the aesthetics of firearms manufacture demonstrated by US weapons of 100 years earlier and present in new guns today – if, in fact, they ever did. There is little doubt, for instance, that certain aspects of the brand-new, Russian-produced Kalashnikov AK74M are backward, ugly and unergonomic. The iron sights, for instance, with the rear sight in the middle of the receiver, represent an ancient concept akin to a late-nineteenth-century rifle – and this is the new Russian military's standard small arm. There simply is no comparison to a modern assault weapon of Western manufacture.

The Second World War was an interesting turning point in the use of small arms as personal weapons. It heralded the large-scale arrival on the battlefield of semi-automatic weapons, now taken for granted by military forces everywhere. Although most sniper rifles are bolt-action (although a few modern models are semi-automatic), personal weapons such as the sub-machine gun reached a never-to-be-repeated level of proliferation during the Second World War.

Typical of the high level of sophistication of the equipment carried by the Axis troops was the German MP40 sub-machine gun, often incorrectly called the 'Schmeisser' (while Schmeisser's Erma-Werke factory built the gun, he didn't design it), a high-quality 9mm weapon whose general design is still present in modern guns. Equally, the Luger was a 1908 design that some shooters still regard as the most beautiful (and complex) handgun ever built. Meanwhile, the more warlike and robust Walther P38, which replaced the Luger in 1942, was one of the pioneers of the double-action trigger unit in a self-loading pistol. The British No. 4 Enfield rifle in .303 calibre was a truly attractive gun, clad from butt to muzzle in wood, and the contentious Sten Mk II has a place in history for being the sub-machine gun that most simply displays the fundamental metal brutality of that type of weapon. All are unique, and all are attractive in their own way.

Had it not been for the exploits of Zaitsev and his snipers, the Mosin Nagant would have been in real danger of dropping into obscurity as a mass-produced weapon that had little to offer a rapidly modernising military world. It's interesting to note that the iron sights on the rifle were even measured in the ancient Russian system of *arshins*, which derive from the length of a human pace. To buy in a live M1891/30 today would cost around £150, whereas a deactivated, field-strippable Sten Mk II or a standard GI-issue American Garand from the Second World War – even an average-condition, non-functional model – could cost as much as £500.

So why the fascination with the Nagant? Largely because it's a classic weapon from a terrible period in human history. It represents, better than any gun we know, the struggle to arm a nation against invaders. This rifle *was* the infantry war in Russia, as the 'T' series of tanks *were* the tracked-artillery war. (Thank you to Paul Greenow for the loan of his beautifully restored example of a 1943 Mosin Nagant for use in this book.)

After the Second World War, the AK47 became king and Mosin Nagants were sold by the Soviets to satellite states for the next forty years. Back in Stalingrad, the stunning use of an old-style rifle in the harshest of combat situations makes the Vasily Zaitsev story all the more amazing.

Finally, it's impossible to discuss Zaitsev without looking at the one period of his war on Germany that has been covered in film and literature more than any other personal, man-on-man conflict in the Second World War: Zaitsev's duel with the German sniper Colonel Heinz Thorwald, a Teutonic super-sniper who was despatched by the German high command to eliminate Zaitsev and destroy not only the man but also the psychological effect he was having on the German troops in Stalingrad.

Popular history would have us believe that Thorwald was the senior instructor at the Zossen sniper school in Germany. A supremely confident man, he was sent to Stalingrad to kill Zaitsev and destroy the stranglehold that the Russian snipers had on the city. There was no question about his ability to succeed; indeed, it was considered a done job, and to call his relationship with Zaitsev a duel is to oversimplify matters. Both men left calling cards in the form of astounding kill shots so that the other would know where they were operating in the city. Their meeting was inevitable, and the German eventually decided to lie up in a prime location for three days, waiting for Zaitsev to show. This was to be their only one-on-one meeting, and it was Zaitsev who allegedly outwitted Thorwald and killed the German with a well-aimed shot into his concealed sniper hole. To both the Russian populace and the German Army, it was this encounter that finally gave Vasily Zaitsev the stuff of immortality. It was the ultimate publicity coup and a resounding, bloody blow to the German invaders.

Whether or not the Thorwald–Zaitsev story is true is irrelevant (conspiracy theories abound). It is for all the wrong reasons that Zaitsev has become such a legend in the world of snipers, and it's not because of this duel that he's earned a place in this book; he should be remembered for what he brought to the world of sniping. He didn't benefit from military training as a sniper, as no such training existed in Russia at the time; he simply adapted the skills he'd learned as a child with a hunting rifle to an urban environment, using them to stalk a different prey. He must have wondered at times whether he was achieving anything, given the magnitude of the battle around him. Little did he know that, by just surviving and deploying the ancient fieldcraft and hunting skills that were to him a natural way of stalking any prey, he was perfecting a new discipline of warfare and taking it to a benchmark level.

We can learn so much about sniping by looking at Vasily Zaitsev and the environment in which he fought. His background, his equipment and his skills as a hunter, developed at an early age, were what made him what he was – a world-class sniper – long before he'd ever caught Heinz Thorwald in his crosshairs.

CHAPTER SEVEN

Monte Cassino – The Allied Stalingrad

'Oh, Christ. Monte Cassino. I remember that.'

Spike Milligan

By December 1943, the Germans had set up the Gustav Line, a defensive line of troops and hardware that spanned the width of the Italian border, to counter the Allied attack.

Cassino became the focus of attack for Allied forces because it protected Highway 6, the main route to Rome. The Americans tried to break through until mid-January 1944, whereupon British and French troops joined the fighting. The roadway most suitable for vehicles bound for Rome, however, stretched over the mountaintop of Monte Cassino. This was a strategic vantage point, not just because of its accessibility for vehicles but also because of its location, on the high ground overlooking the town of Cassino itself.

The peak was deemed a holy place. An ancient abbey had been

founded there by Saint Benedict Nursia in AD 529, allegedly on the former site of the Temple of Apollo, whose original buildings were destroyed by the bombards in AD 580 and rebuilt in AD 720. Monte Cassino was again destroyed in AD 883 by the Saracens and restored in the mid-900s. In 1349, it was damaged by an earthquake, then was rebuilt again in 1600 – only to be brought down once again by the French. It was patiently rebuilt again, whereupon it remained unspoiled until 1944.

During the Second World War, the Germans had 'removed' some holy relics from the monastery on the pretence that they were storing them safely away from potential Allied bombing. Indeed, the Allies did bomb Monte Cassino (under Operation Strangle), but this didn't persuade Nazi Field-Marshal Kessling to retreat from the Gustav Line; instead, the Germans moved into the ruins of Monte Cassino.

General Alexander took over the strategic planning and ordered a major attack, using the British Eighth Army and their American counterparts in an operation codenamed Diadem, which commenced on 11 May 1944. The bloodiest of fighting ensued, in which the Americans lost 1,681 men during the first two days – but this proved to be only the tip of the iceberg; they would soon lose 2,200 more men, while 4,400 British troops would perish.

One of the main reasons for such high numbers of casualties was the effectiveness of the German snipers. In a classic manoeuvre, the Germans took their safest – but all-seeing – position on high ground, within the ruin of the abbey itself, and picked off as many enemy troops as they could as they attempted to scale the sides of the mountain beneath them.

But was it really that simple for the Germans? History books would have us think so, but it has proved to be only the surface of the truth, as veterans of the battle have since disclosed. This book provides an appropriate forum to glimpse under the skin of this 'traditional' sniper action and to appreciate the subtleties of the massacre – because that's what it was, for the British and American troops, as the death count has clearly shown.

One day, a British sergeant whose head was visible above the entrance for a split second was killed by a German sniper lying in wait. All of the German snipers at Monte Cassino had to display this degree of tenacity, as this was the one battle – more so than Stalingrad – in which vigilant watching and opportune sniping would provide the key to victory. But the shooting at Monte Cassino was far from easy; shooting either uphill or downhill requires a greater understanding of the nature of ballistics than shooting on a level trajectory.

Let's assume that we have a Mauser 98K rifle, equipped with a scope zeroed for 300m, which is probably about the range at which the German snipers would have engaged the British troops attempting to climb the steep hill. If the German sniper who killed the aforementioned British sergeant had aimed directly at the target's head, he would have missed; the shot would have travelled over the target. Why? Because rifles shoot high when aimed downhill or uphill. It makes no difference where you're shooting, it just happens. This phenomenon can be explained with resort to trigonometry, but it's a long story involving the use of complex mathematical diagrams. Suffice to say that it's the flying bullet's relationship with the tug of gravity that causes this effect. Gravity affects objects travelling on a horizontal plane differently to how it affects objects travelling at an angle, up or down, the practical upshot being that, at 300m downhill, in order to hit his target, a German sniper would have to zero his gun for a target range of approximately 260m. It's a complicated process but a necessary skill learned by all snipers. In his book *War of the Rats*, David Robbins demonstrates that Vasily Zaitsev was aware of and instructed his pupils in this skill:

You must reason that the wind is blowing unimpeded. Were it humid, or early in the morning after a cold night, you'd need to adapt your aim for those differences as well. Next, you're shooting slightly downhill. Take that into account. The trajectory of your bullet will decay faster and you will undershoot. The opposite is true when you're firing uphill; your bullet will sail and you'll overshoot.

DAVID L ROBBINS, WAR OF THE RATS

The weather, windage and visibility were diabolical. The men who survived the assault on Monte Cassino have admitted to being haunted for the rest of their lives by the horror and sheer terror that they experienced there – horror at seeing their friends and colleagues butchered; terror of not knowing if they would join them, and very soon. Even sixty years later, veterans physically break down in tears when they talk about their plight at Monte Cassino. The nights were pitch black, the rain often heavy, the mud on the mountainside slippery, providing no foothold and consequently no opportunity for a speedy getaway. And yes, as in Stalingrad, there was even snow.

The German snipers were positioned at an altitude of 1,700 feet. Far below them lay the town of Cassino in a Devil's punchbowl of darkness and foreboding. The wind blew fiercely from the sea, but despite this the snipers pulled off an amazing ratio of successful hits and proved, when viewed against the onslaught that they suffered at Stalingrad, that they could use sniper teams as successfully as the Russians. It had been the war of attrition in the freezing cold that had hit the Germans so hard at Stalingrad, as it had Napoleon's army so long before. Monte Cassino was a bloodbath for Allied Forces and served to highlight – to the naïve military mind – the true nemesis of the trained enemy sniper.

Despite the training of snipers by the British during the Great War, the Second World War made it clear that the Germans were at last a match for them, one on one. When the battle was fought by Allied troops against enemy snipers embedded in such an elevated position, however, there was no contest and with hindsight the Allied commanding officer, General Alexander, made a critical mistake sending in row upon row of troops to battle such a focused enemy. History might label this with some justification as the Second World War equivalent of the Charge of the Light Brigade.

> I was blown up at Monte Cassino. That was a hairy battle. We were going to take a mountain when suddenly something exploded and blew me up. I suppose I should have stayed up. When I came to, I was being driven through the lines and I was shaking like mad; I had battle fatigue, and every time there was an explosion, I jumped. And there was this wounded man beside me, his arm in a sling, and every time I jumped, he put his hand on my shoulder and said, 'There now, mate. It'll be alright.' I would like to thank that man.
>
> SPIKE MILLIGAN IN CONVERSATION WITH CRAIG CABELL,
> 3 SEPTEMBER 1999

The lack of information that the British generals of the Great War had at their fingertips is shocking. The quote at the beginning of chapter four, concerning General Haig's Chief of Staff's reaction on witnessing conditions in the trenches, makes this very clear, it's also true of the Second World War and General Alexander's decision to take Monte Cassino. The general's strategic thinking and forward planning was behind the times, but was his approach to warfare any more outdated than that of his enemy?

Montgomery wouldn't have had such a problem, but he had

nothing to do with Monte Cassino. In fact, Montgomery has been criticised much over the years, mainly because he was an egotist, although it's our opinion that his battle dress said it all: he genuinely came through the ranks and, with a little bit of luck, became a general, and one who knew how the men felt and what they needed. Monty was a hero to his own men; he knew trench warfare, and he never forgot the battle scars he received as a subordinate. In short, he had perception.

So, Monte Cassino was important to the growing awareness of the slow-learning generals, statisticians, plotters and strategy-makers. Never again would the British and Americans leave themselves so exposed to the elements and snipers. Through Monte Cassino and Stalingrad, the sniper had come of age and he would not go away. Both tragedies marked the end of the first phase of the military sniper and formed the basis of the second phase: the crack, specially trained sniper.

After such terrible losses at Monte Cassino, the Allies pulled back from their pursuit, although a tenacious troop – the Polish Second Corps – harried the Germans. Indeed, they succeeded where the Allied forces had failed and took the monastery. Although that operation took only three weeks, the death toll was enormous, mostly due to enemy snipers picking off Polish troops as they scaled the slopes beneath the abbey.

On 18 May 1994, Poland celebrated one of its greatest victories of the Second World War against the Germans. Ceremonies were conducted at the Polish cemetery at Monte Cassino to honour the 1,100 Poles who died while storming the abbey between 11 and 25 May 1944.

The campaigns at Monte Cassino and Stalingrad changed the state of warfare for the rest of the twentieth century. No longer would men be wasted so badly. Counter-measures would be more stringent in the future and, most importantly, sniper action would become an important point in any future operation.

During the second half of the twentieth century, the sniper was considered a different beast and trained accordingly. It had taken the military mind only around 150 years from the shot that killed Lord Nelson to realise this.

Life is one long hell.

SPIKE MILLIGAN

CHAPTER EIGHT

The Kennedy Kill

> 'Everyone seems to remember with great clarity what they
> were doing on 22 November 1963, at the precise moment
> they heard President Kennedy was dead.'
>
> FREDERICK FORSYTH, THE ODESSA FILE

We need to start this chapter with an apology. When planning this book, we found that we couldn't avoid writing about President Kennedy and that day in Dallas. Of all the good Kennedy achieved, from the resolution of the Cuban Missile Crisis to the prophetic words that would inspire mankind to journey to the moon, it's always his death that fascinates and generates so much discussion. That is quite unfair. However, because this book concerns snipers, it's fitting that we discuss Kennedy's assassination in a personal way. Indeed, we owe it to his memory to put our theories to the test, because we, the authors, feel that the official version of the events that led to his assassination is wrong.

The one thing we must make very clear from the start is that we believe Lee Harvey Oswald did not kill President Kennedy. That's our opinion. Now let's tackle the important issue: the great sniper shot – or, indeed, shots – taken by a man (or men) who walks in shadows to this day, lacking remorse or boast. It begs the question, who truly can keep their mouth shut after such a world-changing action? Special Forces?

We don't care who killed Kennedy, or for what reason. The fact is that he's dead and, we believe, someone – a sniper or snipers – got away with his murder. We're not concerned with the latest conspiracy theories, just an understanding of the fatal shot(s) and all the preparation that went into it/them. So let's now look at the Kennedy kill from the viewpoint of the book depository, the grassy knoll and wherever else to dispel or confirm what happened to the shots fired and their significance. To do this, we must look carefully at the reaction of the victims of those shots and draw our conclusions.

Let's go back to Dallas, on 22 November 1963. Why was Kennedy there? He was electioneering. His first term [sic] as President was reaching its conclusion; he would have to go to the polls in 1964, so he wanted Dallas onside. For this reason, he toured the city in an open-top car. Let the people see him, be at one with him. Take away the distance created by a pane of glass and a fibreglass roof.

Let's stop there for a moment. How did Oswald know that the President would be in an open-top car? The decision wasn't made that far in advance. From the elevated shooting point of the book depository, Oswald couldn't possibly have hit the President in an enclosed car, so surely he was getting intelligence from somewhere, for him to boldly take an elevated vantage point. [7]

7. This is not to add fuel to any conspiracy theory but merely to add weight to the theory that Oswald was not the shooter.

Moving on from this point, let's locate all our possible snipers and understand the difficulties of killing President Kennedy.

It was a beautiful, sunny afternoon in Dallas, the day's brightness glinting off sunglasses as seductively as from a sniper's scope. But the crowd weren't conscious of such things; they were there to see – to cheer – their President. Yes, there was a carnival atmosphere; the sound was deafening, which probably explains why nobody – no eyewitness – can say with any degree of accuracy what happened that day in Dallas, or from which direction the bullets came.

One thing is for certain, though: the President was shot in the head. The reason why his brain went missing is that the human brain has the same consistency as ballistic gel, which resembles a large block of translucent candle wax. Bullets are fired into it to give a visual representation of how they react when they strike a target. Take for example a bullet designed to fragment; when fired into ballistic gel, it's possible to track through the clear material and in which direction the fragments have broken off in order to determine what sort of wound channels they would make. In short, Kennedy's brain would have shown the trajectory of the bullet(s) and could have been used to prove that Oswald's shot didn't kill the President. We believe that Oswald could have hit the man in front of Kennedy, Governor Connely, but who cares about that poor soul?

OK, let's stay with Oswald for a moment. There he is at the famous window of the book depository with an Italian six-round, Mannlicher-Carcano-model 1938 bolt-action rifle, taking his shots. Now, if he hits Kennedy with his first shot, why isn't the President flung forward in the car? Because the shot is clearly coming from in front of him. Instead, what Kennedy does is put his hands up to his throat *for no apparent reason*. This is a bizarre reaction for a man shot from behind.

Our money is on a similar-distance shot coming from the front, pushing him back into his seat, so naturally his hands would rise up to his throat. Also, crucially, he doesn't appear to move under the force of the round's impact. We believe there's ballistic evidence that supports this theory. Bullets have different 'hitting power' characteristics, depending on how far away the target is from the shooter. If someone was to shoot a live target at a distance of 10m with a single shot from a modern high-velocity, 5.56mm assault rifle, the target would probably sway a little and then turn around and shoot back, as the bullet from this type of gun is travelling so fast that it imparts virtually no energy to the target. Equally, if someone shot the same target at the same range with a .45 ACP pistol round, the poor chap would pitch over and probably wouldn't get up again. This is because the .45 ACP bullet is a low-velocity round, originally designed as a bullet to be used in trench warfare, with a maximum hitting power at around 20 feet, making it ideal for modern law-enforcement officers, who do most of their shooting at close ranges, want to guarantee a 'one-shot stop' and need a bullet with low penetration so as not to kill the target. (This is why there's a slight concern regarding airport police who carry 5.56mm rifles; there's a high probability of close-range shooting, and an equally high probability that the round will pass through two people before it stops!)

Given the ranges of the Kennedy shooting, a round from behind and high up would have transferred energy to Kennedy and thrown him forward; on film, it would have appeared as though he'd been punched very hard on the back of the neck. Conversely, a round from the front would have made Kennedy grab instinctively for the front of his throat and hold him in position as he was forced back into the seat, which is exactly what the Zappruder film shows. [8] The subsequent shots appear to us to come in diagonally, from behind him to both left and right. It's the bullet to Kennedy's right that causes the most damage, but – and this is a big but – the shot on the left side counts, too; the shots are synchronised and coming from too low an angle to have been fired by Oswald. (Was one from the grassy knoll? Does it matter?)

Jackie Kennedy is then seen crawling down the back of the car, not to get away from the fire but to retrieve a part of her late husband's skull, overcome with shock and horror. Don't forget, one moment she's waving to the crowds and laughing with her husband, the next he's lost half his head and blood is pumping all over her. Let's get very real here: this was a professional sniper action. In fact, we believe that it was synchronised sniper shots arriving from different angles.

It's our belief that the President was shot three times: once to the throat – a nervous, early shot of a total of four synchronised shots – and then twice from behind, at a similar angle (i.e. from in the crowd/knoll). (It's possible that Oswald fired the slightly early shot that hit Governor Connely.)

This isn't a conspiracy theory; we're not accusing the American government of a cover-up; we're simply telling you that Oswald knew what was going on, because he was in on the shooting, but he was a pawn in a much bigger game and was shot in order to keep him silent. The whole operation, then, was watertight. Similarly, it's our belief that the other snipers would have been murdered, too, as otherwise one would have uttered a death-bed boast by now.

So there we have it: four synchronised shots to change a Presidential administration. All the snipers killed to keep quiet. Assassination completed. End of story. Now let's start the conspiracy theories.

---

8. This is even evident in the excellent mini-series *Kennedy*, starring Martin Sheen.

Actually, let's not. Let's just assume that Oswald did do it. How, in fact, did he go about it?

First, he scoped his rifle in the back garden of his house in suburbia. Did no one hear him do this? You can't just pick up a scoped rifle and begin to shoot; the weapon must be zeroed for the range at which you want to shoot. If you belong to a gun club with a 200m range, that's the range at which your gun will probably be set, as you'd want to deliver a perfectly flat trajectory at 200m. If you then go to shoot on a 500m range, you'll need to adjust the telescopic sight to make the bullet fly on a different trajectory. Unless you are a highly skilled marksman, you probably won't achieve this on one shot; it might take at least five or six: shoot, adjust, shoot, adjust and so on. Oswald simply could not have done this in his garden, as the entire neighbourhood would have heard. Our conclusion is that Oswald's rifle was pre-sighted to around 100 yards (the distance of the shoot), probably by an expert – perhaps even by one of the other professionally trained shooters we've suggested were involved. Oswald then took the gun, in some kind of disguised format, to the book depository and picked his moment to kill President Kennedy.

So that's the basic story? Forgive us for being flippant, but this scenario doesn't hang together. The gun was waiting for him. It was scoped, loaded and ready to go. He then missed his target (albeit marginally). At least, that's the way we see it.

It's said that Oswald was a good shot. We refuse to get involved in various theories of conspiracies and of people covering their tracks, or to debate whether or not the evidence against Oswald was fabricated; let's just say that he was either nervous, a tree was in the way, he was shooting into the sun, his attention was snared by a distraction, or it was just a bad day at the depository. Whatever happened, Oswald was helped. Somewhere along the line, he had support and, somewhere along the line, he had to be liquidated in order to protect the guilty. But who was the guilty? We don't know, and identifying him or them isn't the purpose of this chapter. What we *do* care about is the Sniper Gauntlet.

Sniper Gauntlet

Whatever happened in Dallas on that bright, sunny, momentous day, a group of people really *knew* that Kennedy wasn't leaving his car alive. Four men with guns were waiting for the President, two of them possibly 'unprofessional' snipers (Oswald, plus whoever delivered the throat shot) and two professionals (the architects of the synchronised head shots). Let's be clinical about this: the quality of the first two shots isn't as good as that of the second two, and itchy, pre-emptive fingers took the unprofessional shots away early. The other two, however, are historic.

Ignoring Oswald's shot, the unprofessional throat shot has come from somewhere close to the President. Indeed, one conspiracy theory has it that the driver did it. OK, that's ridiculous, but we do believe the shot came from *very* close by – if not close enough to be from somebody known to the President, then from somebody shooting from a cunningly disguised sniper den, such as a manhole. And, judging by the angle, the shot must have come from at least standing, crouching or lying level on the street. Here, the grassy knoll and the crowd provide strong possibilities for the killer blows.

We point out the grassy knoll because a police officer was seen running away from it after the assassination. Who is he? Well, that's the million-dollar question. Possibly, he is in disguise to reach his vantage point, like Frederick Forsyth's fictitious Jackal.

So there's one of the killers on screen for you, and possibly one of the most revered snipers of all time.

There is, however, another plausible vantage point for a sniper, one not widely talked about, and that's the railway bridge, well ahead of the motorcade. This would have been an outstanding shooting position, as the sniper would be directly facing the car and the shot would be exponentially easier from a head-on angle. Tracking horizontally something the size of the human head is difficult with any rifle at any range. It is a small target and both skill and luck are often required to keep it dead centre in the crosshairs. But head-on, and from above, a sniper could simply point the gun at the whole target mass – that is, head and body – and let gravity take the muzzle in a smooth downward motion as he tracks the progress of the vehicle.

The only flipside to the theory that the bridge was a sniper's vantage point is that he would be very exposed. There have never been any reported sightings of a shooter on the bridge, but because of the ease of that particular shooting position one could have been deployed and swept away very quickly. No lengthy set-up would have been required if the gun was in relatively experienced hands and the sight calibrated for the approximate distance of a predicted shot. And who would have noticed another Dallas police car or motorcycle in the vicinity? After the President was hit, people would see just another police vehicle speeding away to render aid. Indeed, there has never been any evidence to support the bridge shot, other than the nagging feeling to the experienced shooter that the throat shot comes from somewhere to the front of the car, and this location certainly cannot be discounted as a possible sniper's nest.

As we said earlier, however, this 'guaranteed' kill shot was not achieved; instead, it hit the President in the throat. Of course, this shot probably would have killed him very soon, but had this been the only shot then Kennedy might have survived. So why did the putative 'bridge shooter' not get a direct head shot? Nerves? Or the common mistake that a round fired downhill requires the gun sight to be set differently to a round fired on a flat trajectory? (As mentioned in the previous chapter, gravity can really mess with a bullet, depending on whether it's fired uphill, downhill or along flat to the ground.) Perhaps the scope wasn't correctly adjusted for a downhill shot and the well-aimed (and, frankly, quite easy) shot actually failed to hit the head square-on.

This, of course, is just another theory for the sniper student to chew over, but it challenges the 'sniper-gauntlet' theory and the evidence of the bullets – as shown in the footage – that fly towards the President's head.

So, are we clear in our theory of a sniper gauntlet? Yes. Through our interpretation of the footage, the bridge is the next best option. Are we sure about that? Yes, because if the assassin shot from the bridge, the throat shot would have come from too far a distance and would have caused a much different reaction from Kennedy. It would also have been the second miss from our great sniper (the first miss hitting Governor Connely in the chest – too sloppy for a professional killer) and from the perfect vantage point. However, if four snipers shot four synchronised head shots, then, in terms of accuracy, the Kennedy assassination was only 50 per cent successful.

The assassination of President Kennedy was well planned. Human error was taken into consideration – the magnitude of the job in hand – and the cover-up had to be watertight. That's how accurate, how calculated, how cunning, how cold-blooded the most tenacious sniper (or mastermind) has to be. That's the whole point of this book – the agenda of this book: the anatomy of a sniper is different to that of any other human being. The sniper is a different beast. He is patient, secretive, professional, astute, intelligent. He covers his tracks. Perhaps the three other men we believe were involved in the Kennedy shooting did that, but Oswald didn't. However, he doesn't fit our criteria for a professional sniper. We feel sorry for him, we really do. Perhaps he wanted to kill the President of the United States but the part of him that was a professional shooter compelled him to say, 'Sorry, I missed.' Then what?

Then three other snipers from the sniper gauntlet would come into the frame. But, conveniently, Oswald was killed, and we believe the fantastic stories surrounding the famous incident, like the curse of Tutankhamen. Lord Carnarvon, one of the discoverers of the child-pharaoh's tomb, wanted two doctors at his autopsy, as he feared death through poisoning abroad. As it turned out, only one was present and his stomach removed, so no trace of poison could be made. Now think about the president's brain again...

We don't need conspiracy theorists to tell us something is rotten in the state of Dallas; we can see it for ourselves. We've seen the footage and heard all the evidence against Oswald, but it just doesn't hang together when, it would seem, Kennedy is shot three times from three different angles and the man in front of him is shot once by a fourth shooter – possibly from an open manhole, or maybe by Oswald – all at roughly the same time.

And the magic bullet? Did it really weave in the air? Or have we always had a misconception of the seating arrangements in the car? There was, of course, no magic bullet. This unique round exists simply to support the single-shooter theory. The bullet famously found in the hospital was indeed matched to Oswald's gun, but it was in an unblemished condition, other than the rifling marks inflicted on it as it streaked through the barrel of the gun. The round actually looks remarkably like a test bullet fired into water or some other soft material used by forensic scientists to get a perfect specimen from a gun allegedly used in a crime.

And what of recoil? Even Oliver Stone's numbingly well-researched *JFK* forgot about that factor. That movie portrays

Oswald – played by Gary Oldman – firing his rifle out of the window, proving that the shots could be fired in the time frame given. But what's this? A recoilless gun! It's a huge flaw in Oliver Stone's supposedly accurate film. Oldman is firing blanks, which obviously don't propel the gun back into the shoulder as no projectile is being pushed out of the barrel. Had Oldman been firing live ammunition, the rifle would have been thrust back into his shoulder and the muzzle would have moved skywards at least 9–10cm on every shot. The shooter would then have to reacquire the target through the sight.

Following a recent sniper-rifle shoot involving 7.62mm rounds, we can accurately report first-hand that the first shot from such a rifle is always a bit of a shock, no matter how accustomed you are to shooting. The gun moves a lot in your grip, and for this exercise we were shooting prone on the ground, in some comfort and with modern weapons, while, according to the film *JFK*, Oswald was holding the rifle without any bipod or shooting rest and so would have received the full force of the recoil in his shoulder. Oswald's rifle, the Carcano, has no rubber recoil buffer on the butt like a modern gun and the thump of wood on shoulder is quite severe, making it tough even for a trained sniper to maintain control.

Fortunately, cinema doesn't always get details quite so wrong. In *Dirty Harry*, for example, recoil is effectively demonstrated, and Clint Eastwood's realistic performance gives us a real idea of how difficult the Smith & Wesson Model 29 .44 Magnum is to control, his gun rising impressively after each shot. This is actually quite difficult to act, so the makers were wise to give the principal actor experience of the live gun.

So, by taking this simple characteristic of gun physics – Newton's third law of motion (i.e. for every action, there is an equal and opposite reaction) – into consideration, we open another huge can of worms, especially with regard to *JFK*, and add even more weight to the sniper-gauntlet theory.

Four men were hired to shoot the President. One, we know, didn't get away with it. It's just unfortunate that he was the only one who missed.

He was hit at 12:22 in the afternoon, Dallas time, and the announcement that he was dead came at half past one in the same time zone. It was 2:30 in New York, 7:30 in the evening in London and 8:30 on a chilly, sleet-swept night in Hamburg.

FREDERICK FORSYTH, *THE ODESSA FILE*

CHAPTER NINE

Sniper Research

'Get it first – but first get it right.'
IAN FLEMING, '*FOREIGN NEWS*', IN THE KEMSLEY MANUAL
OF JOURNALISM

When studying snipers, one must cover many different approaches and perceptions in order to explain the many facets of good and bad sniping. To this end, when researching this book, we spoke to many people connected to the police force and various aspects of the armed forces and the defence industry. Although our conclusions are clearly shown in the relevant chapters, we thought it important to tackle the fictional counterpart of the sniper.

In this book, Frederick Forsyth and David L Robbins discuss their own famous works of sniper fiction, while we have also commented on the often inaccurate portrayals on the cinema screen (see Afterword). However, while Craig had been travelling at high speed through the Norfolk countryside with a trained sniper, he was told, 'If you want a great interpretation of a sniper on screen, dedicate a ten-hour movie to a man lying motionless and eventually firing one shot. That's when you'll get the boys saying, "That was pretty accurate, albeit slightly shortened."'

The world of the sniper will never translate well to movie because his work is minimal; it lacks the big build-up, the muck and bullets and several lorry-loads of shells and blood and guts that get him all the way into the inner sanctum of the mastermind: the ultimate enemy. Sometimes, though, good fiction – and, exceptionally, good short fiction – can bridge that time and provide a fantastically suspenseful sniper story. In our view, the greatest short sniper story is Ian Fleming's Bond story *The Living Daylights*. This chapter explains how Fleming did his homework for a story that was absolutely butchered – like most Bond stories – at the cinema (see also David L Robbins's interview concerning the film counterpart to his novel *War of the Rats* in annexe G).

James Bond lay at the five-hundred-yard firing point of the famous Century Range at Bisley. The white peg in the grass beside him said 44 and the same number was repeated high up on the distant butt above the single six-foot-square target that, to the human eye and in the late summer dusk, looked no larger than a postage stamp.

IAN FLEMING, *THE LIVING DAYLIGHTS*

Fleming wrote *The Living Daylights* for the first issue of *The Sunday Times*'s colour supplement in 1962. However, he normally serialised his work in Lord Beaverbrook's *Daily Express* and, when the story appeared, the newspaper magnate was not impressed and axed the Bond cartoon from his paper.

Although probably the greatest short piece of sniper fiction written, *The Living Daylights* didn't endear people to Fleming, and both critics and editors disliked it. The contemporary feel for the story, however, is that it was a little ahead of its time. It was published in book form only after Fleming's death in 1964, as a slim, double-handed volume, along with another Bond story *Octopussy*, by Jonathan Cape in 1966.

Of *The Living Daylights* and *Octopussy* (joined by *Property of a Lady* in subsequent editions), the former is the stronger, mainly because it evokes that effortless research that Fleming used to inject into his best long fiction. Obviously, for *The Living Daylights*, that research concerns firearms.

In the December 2004 issue of *Book & Magazine Collector*, a news feature appeared concerning the auction of unpublished letters to and from Fleming written during the time he was creating Bond. The highlight of the collection concerns correspondence with Geoffrey Boothroyd, a Glaswegian gun expert who, shortly after reading the first Bond novel, *Casino Royale*, wrote to Fleming explaining that the gun used by Bond (a .25 Beretta) was completely wrong for such a character. [9] Fleming, always wise to employ intellect, made Boothroyd his paid adviser on arms-related matters. He also fictionalised him as 'the Armourer' ('Q'), Major Boothroyd, in *Dr No* (Jonathan Cape, 1956), one of his finest Bond novels.

However, Fleming was no shrinking violet; he had been in Naval Intelligence during the Second World War (as he mentioned in his excellent non-fiction book *Thrilling Cities*) and wasn't afraid of action, as actor Christopher Lee related to Craig in 1994: 'There

9. On 4 November 2004, the letters sold at Bloomsbury Auctions for £44, 750, more than double their estimated value. At the same auction, a first edition of *From Russia With Love*, signed and inscribed 'To Geoffrey Boothroyd. Herewith appointed "Armourer" to J. Bond from Ian Fleming', made £22,750 (estimated £4,000, 5,000 – a world-record price. Meanwhile, a first edition of *Dr No*, also signed to Boothroyd, also made a world-record-breaking price of £19,450.

was an awful lot of James Bond in Ian: a man who could be privy to secrets and not give them away, attractive to women and certainly they to him. He was also very good at sports and swept the playing fields at Eton.'

Fleming was a quick learner, and in October 1961 he offered a Boothroyd-inspired article to *The Sunday Times* entitled 'The Guns of James Bond', but it was rejected by the editor on the grounds that it was too long. Ironically, it was only on this rejection that Fleming wrote *The Living Daylights* – a heavily gun-related piece – and fell out with Lord Beaverbrook. Rumour had it that Beaverbrook believed that Fleming wrote only fiction for him and non-fiction for *The Sunday Times* (not unlike his articles that went into making *Thrilling Cities*), but Fleming didn't appreciate this and therefore the mistake – and it *was* a genuine mistake – was made.

The Living Daylights was originally drafted under the title *Trigger Finger*, the codename of the female sniper in the story. Fleming's choice to give 'Trigger' a Kalashnikov is in itself worthy of comment. Bond takes in the enemy weapon as it slips out of the darkness: 'He strained his eyes, taking in the squat flash eliminator at the muzzle, the telescopic sight and the thick downward chunk of the magazine. Yes, that would be it! Absolutely for sure – and the best they had!'

This quote really dates the story. When *The Living Daylights* was written, of course, the AK47 was a relatively new weapon. It would be another forty years before it would become the most prolific small arm on the planet and, to many non-government organisations, the symbol for all that's bad in the world of the gun; it wasn't until the turn of the twenty-first century that an eminent academic would state that the most dangerous weapon in the world today was an adolescent African male with an AK47. Back in 1965, the Kalashnikov AK was a radical new weapon, capable of accurate fire over 200–300m. It was one of the first assault rifles, a new creature to be feared and a worthy adversary to Bond's .308 Winchester.

The Living Daylights was written quickly, but not rushed. In October/November 1961, Fleming bought a map of Berlin and contacted the National Rifle Association (NRA) in the US, requesting information concerning the Bisley range, where his story began. By mid-November, Captain EK Le Mesurier, secretary of the NRA, had assisted Fleming, not just by answering his questions but also by reading and proofing the manuscript.

An example of Le Mesurier's assistance can be found near the beginning of the story. Fleming had originally written, 'He gave half a turn to a screw on the fixed stand on which his rifle rested. He watched the crossed lines on the Sniperscope move minutely to the right of the bull, to its right-hand bottom corner.' However, Le Mesurier advised that the following could be an option: 'He set two clicks more right on the wins gauge and transversed the crossed wires back on to the point of aim.' Le Mesurier had pointed out that the basic technique Fleming had used was not correct for setting a sniper's scope. To ensure accuracy, a sniper's scope had to be set off line of the barrel in order to allow for wind. This was – or, rather, could have been – a very basic flaw in Fleming's story, but he had the right combination of experts on-side to ensure that the story was pinpoint accurate, and the end result was one of the most pleasing of fictional sniper stories, not just for any James Bond fan but also for any sniper student who enjoys a good story for which a writer has done his research well.

CHAPTER TEN

The Washington Sniper?

John Allen Muhammad, accompanied by his young nephew Lee Malvo, killed thirteen people in what the media labelled 'America's worst sniper case on record'. The killings started on the evening of 2 October 2002 and, as the death toll increased, the world chilled at the unseen enemy. The sniper had ceased to be the stuff of military tales; he was in America's backyard.

During the writing of this book, we were granted an interview with Charles Moose, the Montgomery County Police Chief responsible for tracking down the 'sniper'. Moose had written his own book concerning the incident, *Three Weeks in October: The Hunt for the Washington Sniper* (Orion, 2004), and we welcomed the opportunity to interview him in order to voice our doubts. Was this, in fact, really a sniper incident? We believed that the 'Washington Sniper' wasn't a sniper at all, but a gunman. But is there a difference? We decided to ask Moose some questions and get some hard answers.

This interview is represented here in a question–answer style so that the important questions are clear, as are their direct answers. In truth, we did change our perception as to the definition of a sniper – at least, a sniper in the eyes of the law. And that is the important question to be answered in this chapter, not necessarily the detail of the mechanics of the hunt itself.

Charles Moose: Some people have a military view on the world, and a true military sniper doesn't want these guys [Muhammad and Malvo] associated with them. The military take the more philosophical line that a sniper is there to save lives, as [opposed to] randomly take lives. A military sniper should be there for the greater good, so it will be interesting the way you guys are going to approach this.

Craig Cabell: OK, so what's your definition of a sniper?

CM: Anybody who shoots somebody from a distance and does it in an accurate fashion.

CC: But that opens up the question that the Washington Sniper wasn't shooting at any significant distance to be deemed a classic sniper.

CM: From a technical standpoint, no, but a classic crime would be: I'm mad at you so I'm going to pull out a gun and shoot you. [The police] are used to close-combat homicide.

So you can look at it from a classic sniper point of view, but I'm looking at it from a classic crime point of view. There was a distance, and the person killed didn't even see their assassin, so we're comfortable calling it a sniper.

Richard Brown: So the bulk of the homicides that you dealt with are more akin to handgun crime? Close range?

CM: Not to say that they don't use long guns – that's very rare – but yes, close range.

RB: It's interesting, coming from our perspective, because the classic definition of a sniper is far removed from the Washington Sniper; he wouldn't leave notes, doesn't want to be found and would never make any attempt to contact anyone. Could you tell us who first apportioned the title 'sniper' to this guy?

CM: It was media-driven, because we were very hesitant to call it something without really knowing what we were dealing with, but in order to report the story there is a challenge to frame it in something. So, inaccurately or accurately, [he] was labelled as a 'sniper'.

CC: But how did you relate it to your guys on the street?

CM: More of a serial murder. It became clear that it was the same people – the same weapon, at least – so the serial part makes sense. But the sniper part is really a framework, a reference.

RB: OK. But I think, to the general populace, 'sniper' is a terrifying term, because it does convey somebody you don't know is there.

CM: And that was true in this case.

RB: It's a psychology people can understand.

CM: You have to keep it 'gunman' and keep it generic. It was a clear day and [the shots] came from an unknown distance... There were some shots from wooded areas, and it was only towards the end that we knew that they were shooting from the car.

CC: When did you realise that this case was going to be something quite sinister?

CM: From the Monday they shot the school kid [Iran Brown]. That was when I sent a letter to the Attorney General, asking him to designate it a federal serial murder case, to bring in a lot more resources. Because on that Thursday, that hell day when they did all that shooting, we were hoping that sooner or later we would drive up on this crazed maniac in the middle of an intersection with all of his clothes off, sweating profusely, but the day ended and the crazy person was still out there.

Then you start to think that somebody is doing this methodically rather than just flipped out. And then the whole process of terrorist activity came to our attention, because we had nothing to go on. The common criminal tends to give you something, [although this] did develop later, with the notes and phone calls.

CC: What was the major turning point for you in this case?

CM: Certainly the notes, but it was like a puzzle. The pieces started to come together gradually.

CC: But you still had a lot of hoax calls to try and throw you off the scent?

CM: People don't seem to understand that you have all these loonies who call in to confess. And it's kind of frustrating because you try and explain that to the media and they don't appreciate that you have to hold certain things back. They say, 'Why don't you tell us how many time he was stabbed? [*sic*]', and you don't want to say because a loony will confess, 'Five times,' when the answer is really 500. Only the person who stabbed, and the officers on the case, will know.

RB: But you did issue a public statement about the weapon. And I'm sure that there are people out there who own .223 weapons. That was a calculated gamble for you, surely?

CM: Right. But the key there was to stir things up a little... When I showed a .223, you had a visual, and people would come forward...but there were more .223s in Montgomery County than we ever imagined!

CC: But the media can hinder or they can support. There has to be a balance there.

CM: Yeah. And clearly, although they remain upset that I got upset with *them*, they were far more helpful than they were harmful... They gave the public quality updates, help lines and other important stuff like that.

CC: Let's talk about the notes left by the shooter, because it was the first time you had evidence that more than one person was involved.

CM: Yeah, that's right, but we didn't know if that was somebody trying to be smart. We'd processed that it could have been more than one person involved. We thought that, if it was two people, it could have been a man and a woman, because we felt that two men would fight over the shot, while maybe a man and a woman wouldn't. A woman could be submissive and say, 'I don't need to shoot.' So we were looking at every scenario, from the lone gunman to the man/woman team. But, then again, when he started writing 'we' in his notes, we didn't know if that was just camouflage for the lone gunman. Again, the media got involved and said that they needed to see the notes because somebody recognised the handwriting. That was interesting, but we were thinking, Why wouldn't the person write it with his left hand instead? How would you then recognise the handwriting?

RB: You actually say that the handwriting is quite shaky.

CM: Well, people normally cut out the letters for a ransom note and stick them on a piece of paper, but [Muhammad and Malvo] didn't do that.

CC: You said that you were very disappointed in the end that it was all just about money. Did you really feel that this could have been terrorist activity?

CM: If you and I are neighbours and I regularly urinate in your yard and throw rocks at your window, eventually you will kill me. And people, although they will realise that my life is valuable, will appreciate why you killed me. The people who died at the hands of the sniper hadn't hurt anybody. They weren't hanging out in a prostitute zone or using drugs or stealing, and we constantly look for some rationale for these terrible crimes, but with the only rationale being money. I believe that he had our attention when he killed one person, so why didn't he ask for the money right away?

He didn't need to kill ten people to convince us he was dangerous, or to kill four people in one day.

Now, if they felt that they needed one good day to make us believe they were serious, why did they keep killing afterwards?

CC: Was the case an anti-climax for you because of that aspect? And perhaps because of the superficial way you felt the President thanked you for the final arrests? [10]

CM: No. We received overwhelming gratitude. The community was very responsive. We went to an elementary school and every kid in the school would stand and applaud for thirty minutes, which is unheard of... High-school kids hate the police.

You can respect people for doing something they really believe in. Sometimes you wish they wouldn't go to the extreme... If you're in the National Guard, you'll say, 'I'm willing to die for my country,' and the people who flew the planes into the World Trade Center, they were also willing to do that. They weren't just planting a bomb and running away.

But with the gunman and his partner, just to do all that for money... Well, I'm convinced none of us will ever have enough money. All the money Bill Gates has got, he's just trying to get more. So what makes these guys think they're ever going to get enough? It's an empty goal.

CC: How do you work out this case in your own mind?

CM: It's just a sad case – somebody trying to manipulate the system and take a short cut. You have to balance that perception, because

10. A phone call came in from the President of the United States, who thanked Moose and his team, but there was no intercourse, just a message of thanks that Moose mentioned in his book might as well have been recorded.

there's a camp out there who has a theory that he was going to kill his ex-wife next and then go and claim his kids. I don't really believe that... I say, 'That doesn't look like a guy lining up to be father of the year to me, because he's living in homeless shelters and places like that.' If you're father of the year, you're working three jobs, you got the house, you got the rooms all furnished and the kids' names on their doors. You're just waiting for the moment to get custody of them, right? How's he going to provide for those kids?

RB: To take a different tack now, the sniper is as much psychological weapon as he is physical weapon. What was the psychological effect of the Washington Sniper on the county?

CM: It was devastating. That was why we processed the fact that terrorists train snipers to shoot congressmen on the golf courses of America... and real terrorists wouldn't leave notes. Can you imagine the effect? And with the Washington Sniper, we had notes and other stuff, but gas sales were down and business in the strip malls was down. We were even on the verge of closing the schools.

RB: Were you getting to the stage where people were parking their cars directly outside their office and running in?

CM: Obviously, the people who had underground parking used it. If people had a spouse who worked in a risk area, they'd change their own schedules to ensure that they arrived safely. In some cases, they would take their partner to an underground car park, pay the attendant, drop off their loved one and leave without leaving the car there, because they then had to go to work themselves.

There were no football games, no soccer matches. And then people said, 'We really want the football games, so we're gonna drive eighty miles and have the game on a military base.' The military bases were some kind of sanctuary. If people had ID to get on a military base, they'd go there and buy their gas, even if it was fifty miles out of their way.

RB: But that suddenly falls within the anatomy of a sniper, doesn't it? How one man can terrorise the population of a county?

CC: It's a bit like the horror movie where you're more scared of the monster you can't see.

CM: Right, which is why the Washington Sniper does hit classic definitions: you can't see him, you can't hear him and he terrorises five million people across two states. The fear was just awesome.

The above interview with Charles Moose proved one thing: that the classic perception of the sniper isn't always accurate. We fully admit to arranging the interview with the aim of proving that John Allen Muhammad was nothing more than a nut with a gun who had basic shooting skills. The ranges involved weren't that long; most competent shooters could have achieved similar shots, and the gun he was using was nothing more than a civilian version of the standard US assault rifle – accurate to 200m without a scope. Even the .223 (5.56mm) calibre was wrong – lethal, yes, but not the choice of any trained sniper; it's too light to be considered a viable sniper bullet, as there's too much chance that the target will survive a single shot, and the round can't penetrate body armour. To kill as many people as he did with a .223, Muhammad got lucky. Had he been trained as a professional sniper, he would almost certainly have selected a 7.62mm rifle or larger. Conclusion: anyone reasonably proficient with a modern rifle could have killed all of the Washington victims. So was he a sniper?

Without doubt, yes. What we failed to fully appreciate, before we met Charles Moose, was the impact the shooter had on the American psyche and, more drastically, on the inhabitants within the killing ground. The real sense of horror was lost on UK news coverage. We were exposed to two-minute film clips before we were then ushered on to the next subjected. It was just another tragic story of gun crime from across the Atlantic.

Talking to Charles Moose, however, brought that horror home. It was like meeting the super-sniper sent to Stalingrad to kill Vasily Zaitsev. For a short period in October 2002, Moose was a sniper hunter, his weapon not a 7mm Mauser 98K but the law. By pressing Moose on details, it became very apparent that Muhammad and his colleague did indeed fill one of the key military objectives expected of fully trained snipers: they generated fear in the heart of the 'enemy' and brought chaos to order.

The parallels are inescapable. It doesn't matter whether you're crouched in a fox hole in Normandy in 1944 or exiting a Chrysler Le Baron, shielding your child as you run for the school door; your thoughts are the same: Is he there? Are his crosshairs zeroed on the side of my head? Will I hear it? What will I feel if he gets me?

These are real questions, hard questions that are normally asked only in self-analysis when deep in the heart of combat, not on a school run. The sheer terror generated by the Washington Sniper is sobering. In a world where we're facing new weapons directed at civilians who have committed no crime other than that of living in a certain country, you have to ask yourself why the sniper hasn't been more widely used as a method of instigating terror. One can only imagine how much worse the Washington incident would have been if Muhammad had been a trained military sniper and not just a deranged man who wanted money.

On 9 March 2004, US judge LeRoy Millette sentenced John Allen Muhammad to death, describing the shootings as being 'so vile that they were almost beyond comprehension'.

Muhammad denied any involvement in the shooting, stating, 'Just like I said at the beginning, I had nothing to do with this, and I'll say again, I had nothing to do with this.'

> Here we are now going to the West Side,
> Weapons in hand as we go for a ride.
> MOBY, '*SOUTH SIDE*'

In October 2005 John Allen Muhammad began defending himself in the Washington Sniper case. He is charged with murder, terrorism, conspiracy and firearms offences.

He opened on 21 October by stating that all he wanted was the truth. 'Something happened [referring to his killing spree],' he said. 'Jesus said, "You shall know the truth".' He drew a parallel with a tale of his daughter stealing cookies, his resulting punishment and the defence of her brother who supported his sister but did not actually witness the theft. Muhammad argued that the jury could not know the truth as they were not present when the shots rang out. He insisted they must listen to his side of the story and not pre-judge him.

In true journalistic speak, 'the trial continues'.

CHAPTER ELEVEN

Sniping in the Occupied Territories

In this chapter, rather than taking a single person or major war as our subject matter, we look at a more subtle form of 'sniping', one that doesn't necessarily affect or bother the Western world, although it does provide some interesting sniper-related observations.

On the morning of Sunday 3 March 2002, a fortified and heavily defended Israeli Army checkpoint near Ramallah was attacked. Not by youths armed with shattered pieces of rubble or, at the other end of the military spectrum, by a highly trained mobile assault team brandishing assault rifles and rocket-propelled grenades. Instead, the checkpoint was attacked by a lone Palestinian sniper who successfully targeted and killed seven Israeli soldiers and wounded another five before fleeing into the urban war zone of the region. To add insult to injury, forensic experts later determined that the sniper wasn't using a modern, rapid-fire sniper rifle but an old bolt-action carbine.

On 17 February 2003, outside the Church of the Nativity in

Bethlehem, twenty-four-year-old Israeli Army Captain Shahar Shmul decided to take a closer look at a deserted car. He was carrying the latest military equipment and was armed with a modern 5.56mm assault rifle. He was a seasoned, professional soldier well placed to deal with all military eventualities, and he no doubt feared that an abandoned car in this location might be a booby trap. In fact, it was, but not as Captain Shmul had anticipated. A Palestinian sniper had used the vehicle as a range marker, possibly hours before, and was quietly waiting for an Israeli soldier to walk into his field of fire. Without warning, a single, high-velocity round pierced Captain Shmul's neck, probably just above the protective flange of his ballistic body armour. It's doubtful that he even heard the shot that killed him.

In a war of attrition, where one side massively outweighs the other in military hardware, these and numerous other cases are salutary lessons to those who would dismiss the devastating power of a determined sniper, the one man who can bring an army to its knees and make seasoned soldiers too afraid to walk in the open.

Rarely does a battle flow in one direction, especially when the two sides use snipers. The sniper is the great leveller. This is perhaps why the Palestinians have embraced the art of sniping. Either that or the cases described above are simply return fire from one of the most dangerous military units of all time, the Israeli Defence Force (IDF).

The IDF has never been a typical army. When it formed in 1948, its members initially equipped themselves on very little money and had to deal with a degree of geographic ostracism – which, in fact, still exists today. They focused on highly mobile mechanised assaults – a doctrine still typical of the Israeli armed forces today – and gave very little time to the sniper. It was a luxury they simply could not afford. Any early sniping work (which was often a euphemism for assassination) was carried out by S13 (Shayetet 13), a Marine-based unit trained by the US Navy SEALs.

Until the 1970s, the IDF used any surplus weapons it could find. These weren't necessarily poor weapons, but most of the global sniping community had long since moved away from the vintage firearms used in the 1939–45 conflict and were ushering in a new generation of weapons that would be the staple arms for troops throughout the Cold War. A snapshot of the IDF sniper arsenal in the 1960s would have shown a large number of .303 British Lee-Enfield No. 4 (T) rifles and, ironically, a substantial number of German Mauser 98K rifles, still with their winged-eagle and swastika stampings. Needless to say, some of these guns sat a little uneasily against the cheeks of Israeli sharpshooters, but they liked the weapon and appreciated the functionality of what had been a good military rifle for many years, albeit of German manufacture. The ever-resourceful IDF soon began to seek alternative 98Ks from Czechoslovakia so that their troops were spared the ignominy of having to carry arms bearing Nazi emblems.

When Israel entered the Six-Day War in the 1960s, France had become its primary weapons supplier. As the short war concluded, France and most of its European partners became uncomfortable with continuing to supply weapons to Israel, and the country then had to find a new friend. They turned instead to the USA, whose leaders decided to take advantage of their country's large Jewish population and a wave of national sympathy, and so began one of the closest defence-equipment relationships of our time. Today, it is still a benchmark for others.

The relationship came to fruition in 1973, when the Israelis and Arabs clashed once again in the Yom Kippur War. The US sent a massive weapons-aid package to the embattled Israelis which was to establish a public image for Israeli soldiers for years to come: the IDF soldier armed with a US M16.

However, the arrival of several thousand old American M14 rifles in 7.62mm calibre is of more interest to us. Accurised M14s had been used as sniper rifles by US forces in the Vietnam War, and this unique weapon was designated the M21. The M14 is a robust, well-made weapon still held in high esteem today by US soldiers, who use it in combat, and is currently manufactured for the US civilian and law-enforcement markets by Springfield Armouries. Along with the FN FAL, the AK47 and the Heckler & Koch G3, it is one of the world's great 7.62mm rifles.

The M14 arrived at just the wrong time for the Israelis to put it to combat use, for, along with the shipment of M14s, came a batch of relatively new M16 rifles. Armed forces the world over were switching to the new, fast and light 5.56mm round, and at this time the Israelis were developing their own 5.56mm rifle, the Galil, based on the Russian Kalashnikov and the Finnish Valmet. Combat rounds of 7.62mm had since become old news, but the Israelis had never been those to waste a good weapon and, out of the 35,000 M14s delivered to the IDF, 10,000 were selected as having better-than-average accuracy and were pulled aside to be converted into dedicated sniper rifles – just as the US had done in Vietnam. Fitted with an EL-OP 6x40 scope and packing the newly developed Sierra M852 bullet, the reconfigured M14 at last gave the IDF its first good sniper weapon.

Of course, in keeping with their tradition of self-reliance, the IDF then had to develop its own sniper rifle, and they achieved this by effecting alterations to the standard Galil assault rifle.

Taking a sidestep for a moment, the Galil rifle offers an insight into Israeli military doctrine. Very few countries keep and use semi-automatic sniper rifles. Bolt-action rifles, which deliver only one shot until the mechanism is manually operated, are considered the best option for sniper rifles, but the Israelis insisted on the retention of semi-automatic fire. The existence of this sniper rifle clearly shows how important it was – and, indeed, is – to the IDF to have the ability to lay down sustained fire on a target. This can be seen in the method of their attack, which clearly shows their deeply held belief that massive firepower will ultimately triumph.

This design of the Galil rifle is almost as telling as the selector level on the Kalashnikov AK47 and later models of the same gun, as it moves from safe mode to fully automatic and then to semi-automatic. The idea is that, if its user finds himself in a situation where he has to move his gun from its 'safe' position – i.e. in order to use it – he might immediately need a high rate of fire. Should the shooter wish to use a more moderate approach, however, he simply has to push the selector level down to the next notch. Better to have firepower first and not need it than need it and not to have it immediately to hand. This is completely the opposite of the design concept behind most modern guns, which almost universally have selector levers or switches that can be switched from safe to semi-automatic to sustained fire, rather than going straight from safe to fully automatic.

However, the major drawback that the Israelis found with the Galil sniper model was its weight – an arm-numbing 18.3lb when scoped and loaded. The Galil sniper was never really well received by the IDF, but the weapon is still made and exported today. The US M14 (or M21), however, was a superb, battle-proven firearm. Nevertheless, it wasn't until the 1990s, following particularly heavy losses, that the IDF realised that it had never given sniping – or, more precisely, precision shooting – the attention it deserved, and that long-range surgical bullets could solve more of their battle problems than sending troops by the truckload into highly dangerous situations.

In 1997, the IDF made the changes they hoped would bring their sniping skills into line with, and perhaps beyond, other armed forces. These changes were listed in the following order in an IDF publication.

The standard-issue sniper rifle – the M14 – was replaced by the US M24, a Remington 700 US sniper rifle equipped with a Leopold M3 10x day optic and with an internal five-round magazine. This rifle has now become the standard-issue rifle for all IDF snipers. The move back to bolt-action with the M24 suggests that the IDF sniper might be coming of age. Out went the old mentality of multiple shots with reasonable accuracy in order to support troops; in came the otherwise universally accepted technique of firing single, supremely accurate shots at high-value targets.

The flipside of the IDF receiving the bolt-action M24 was that they genuinely could no longer provide high-speed fire support, which they could have done with the M14 and to which the troops in the streets of Hebron had been accustomed. This tactic had been in IDF doctrine for many years, and to pull it away left the ground troops with a sense of uneasiness. The solution was to create a new profession in the standard military unit: the Designated Marksman.

The IDF Designated Marksman project began in the late 1980s and was then based on using an M16 assault rifle fitted with an El-Op Eyal 3x day optic and a bipod. However, by cutting yet another corner, the IDF failed to give the Marksmen a dedicated command structure, and so the project was doomed. The shooters identified soon merged back into their units as their training was left unmaintained and the Dedicated Marksmen became little more than good shots in the unit.

Realising the error of their ways and finally accepting the fact that armed forces need snipers, the IDF decided to create specially trained snipers (those who were good shots up to 1,000m), who would be supported at unit level by trained marksmen (good up

Above: Range firing the Accuracy International L96A1 at a man-sized target at 100m.

Below: Shooter taking a long look down an H&K MSG90.

'The Death of Nelson' by Arthur William Devis. This famous painting is inaccurate as it shows Lord Nelson's wound on the wrong shoulder.

Lord Nelson's coat as worn at the Battle of Trafalgar. Note the bullet hole in his left shoulder.

Above: Three great modern sniper rifles. *From back*: Accuracy International 7.62mm, H&K PSG1 and MSG90.

Below: Two 1943 combat rifles. Mosin Nagant (*above*) and a Lee Enfield. Note how the cocked bolt of the Enfield permits the attachment of a scope whilst the upward handle of the Nagant had to be changed to fit a sight.

Above: An M16 5.56mm clone, similar to the standard assault rifle used by John Allen Mohammed to create chaos in Washington DC.

Below: Charles Moose, the man behind the successful conclusion of the Washington Sniper case.

Above: An 'accurised' H&K G3 7.62mm assault rifle renamed the SG1.

Below: Vasili Zaitsev (*far left*), hero of the Soviet Union, with the Mosin Nagant sniper rifle.

B L Montgomery of El Alamein.

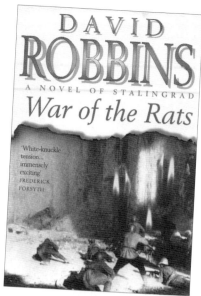

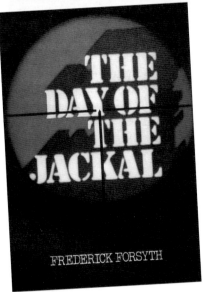

Above left: David L Robbins, author of *War of the Rats*.

Above right: First UK edition of the novel *War of the Rats*, which inspired the movie *Enemy at the Gates*.

Below left: The collectable first UK edition of Forsyth's *The Day of the Jackal*.

Below right: Frederick Forsyth, author of *The Day of the Jackal*.

to 500m). The new Designated Marksman project, in a support capacity, was more of a success, and today the system is highly effective in all units, including civilian defence forces.

Not wishing to leave any stone unturned, the IDF then introduced the Barrett M82A1 HTI (Hard Target Interdiction) anti-matériel rifle. In theory, the M82A1 could also have been used for high-impact sniping (well over 1,000m) against human targets, although it's far better deployed as a weapon for piercing low-level vehicle armour or for disposing of explosive ordnance. (Sniping is often the quickest and easiest – if not the safest – way to remove an anti-personnel mine or terrorist package.)

The introduction of the Designated Marksman into the IDF gave the fully trained Israeli sniper the ability to reach the level of importance most other snipers enjoy in their countries' armed forces. They now had time to move away from unit activities and be fully trained. They could become the best of the best at their trade, not just good shots in a battalion. As sniper staff became available for the first time, a regimented selection process had to be created.

Here the IDF system showed its newness, perhaps its weakness, by not taking the selection process or training seriously. It takes around fourteen months to train an IDF infantry soldier, while it takes about twenty months to train an IDF Special Forces operative. However, the mandatory service for an IDF soldier is only three years. With twenty months of that time taken to train a spec-ops soldier, it's not altogether surprising that unit commanders are reluctant to send their best soldiers off for a further five weeks of sniper training (which, incidentally, is a fairly short sniper course). Therefore, the sniper school received only the misfits: the soldiers who couldn't form relations with unit staff and were better suited to the position of loner, or those who had sustained injuries severe enough to make them of limited value in high-speed street fighting. This is not the way to create an elite sniper unit. Here the mix is all wrong, and here is where one of the world's great fighting forces found itself with a weak link in the chain. A sniper is not a luxury item in modern military set-up; it is an essential commodity, and time and money must be invested in order to generate a high-quality end product. By all accounts, the IDF still aren't prepared to do this with their own soldiers.

So how do the IDF train their snipers? The first thing that's apparent on arriving at the school is that a large number of the instructors are females who have little or no combat experience, while the remainder of the instructors are male soldiers who, for a variety of poor reasons, cannot serve in the regular army. Indeed, the position of sniper instructor in the Mitkan Adam School is considered a very good one, allegedly for the following reasons:

- Mitkan Adam is located in a lovely forest near the centre of Israel, less than a thirty-minute drive from Tel-Aviv, which is handy for travelling home for the weekend.
- The accommodation is well built rather than the rude tents found in many infantry bases.
- The food is good.
- All trainees are given CAR15s (the carbine version of the M16A1), just like combat soldiers.
- Trainees are paid the same as combat soldiers.
- The base has a high number of other soldiers to perform all the chores – guarding, kitchen duties, etc – as regular soldiers also carry out their basic training at the facility.
- Finally, trainees get to go home every weekend, and there are dozens of young female instructors on site. (Bear in mind that IDF soldiers are on average between eighteen and twenty-one years of age!)

All of this paints a fairly flippant and bleak picture of sniping in the IDF, but there are many who suspect – as we considered earlier – that the Israelis deeply believe that they need men on the ground, patrolling the streets, rather than lying up for hours, waiting for the right target – which might never show. Palestinian soldiers, after all, aren't always readily obvious in the same way that a communications officer or a senior officer is in a regular army. Picking your target is hard.

On 13 April 2003, an Israeli sniper shot and killed a British activist who was attempting to rescue a child from a field of fire. An Israeli Army investigation reported that IDF troops opened fire only once in that area on that day. Their target was an armed Palestinian who had previously shot at an outpost.

Tom Hurndall was a member of an eight-man team from the International Solidarity Movement (ISM), a non-governmental organisation that employs non-violent methods to hinder Israeli movements. His wasn't the safest job imaginable, but was he in the wrong place at the wrong time, or was he the victim of a sniper who broke one of the aforementioned golden rules (e.g. never give away your position unless the target is high value and you have an escape route)? The shot that killed Tom allegedly came from a distant high tower – not a good choice for a sniper nest if you want an easy escape route. And Tom certainly was not a high-value target.

Interestingly, though, a spokesman for the ISM said that Tom had been wearing a bright jacket adorned with reflective strips, as had two other members of the organisation who had been killed only weeks earlier: one shot after a curfew and the other crushed by an armoured vehicle. Could these shootings really be the actions of members of a professional military force who knew that they would face investigation for the alleged illegal shootings of foreign civilians? Or was there someone else in the Occupied

Territories taking sniper shots? Are there 'highly trained' shooters in the area making up for Israel's inadequacies in sniping and not really caring who they shoot? Are there sniper secondees to the IDF with the remit of sending a message to others to keep out?

For many months in 2004, there were reports of seasoned Russian snipers who had fought in Chechnya now operating in the West Bank and Gaza. Russian soldiers are apparently filling the ranks of a special sniper unit of the IDF called the Aliya (Immigration) squad. According to an unnamed security official in the IDF, these highly trained snipers are used to fortify 'weak points' in the occupied territory.

Russia gives its snipers years of training, and the IDF knows this. The Russian snipers, meanwhile, are poorly paid and have little loyalty to a country that seems to care little for them. The IDF also knows that its own sniper system is fundamentally flawed, and so, in an effort to keep their own men on the streets and still have an elite sniper unit, it has simply bought in the expertise. In other words, it employs private military operatives. Mercenaries.

Given the horrific reports that have come out of Chechnya, combined with the fact that the immigrant Russian snipers are effectively answerable to no one, is it not surprising that unauthorised shootings do take place? Equally, when an investigation is called, the IDF tends not to draw attention to the fact that it has a squad of renegade Russian snipers in the Occupied Territories, taking 1,000m-plus-range shots at whoever they judge to be a legitimate target.

But what of the Palestinians, who now have to face not only the might of the Israeli Army but also snipers from the Eastern Bloc? They, too, have begun to embrace sniping as a method of war. If the IDF's weakness is a lack of momentum in its creation of an elite sniper unit, the Palestinians' is lack of weapons and ability to train.

Palestinian sniper training is very basic, but as of the late 1990s they have made a concerted effort to formalise what little they have, rather than showing a teenager how to shoot a 9mm handgun in a basement. A report in the newspaper *Ha'aretz* quoted a high-ranking IDF officer, who revealed, 'The Palestinian security forces have recently accelerated and intensified their training... in the use of formations [such as teams and squads] for defined missions.' He is also quoted as stating that the IDF knows 'that the Palestinians are training for combat and aspiring to be able to use anti-tank missiles'. Other reports claim that the Palestinians are seeking expertise on matters such as gaining control of an area and then denying access to it. They are becoming skilled in Close-Quarter Battle (CQB) and have sought professional training in small-arms and hand-to-hand combat.

The Palestinian forces have now embraced the concept of sniper training, and one could argue that they seem more committed to fostering an indigenous capability than the IDF itself. In several confrontations, IDF personnel have witnessed Palestinians carrying Kalashnikov- and M16-style assault rifles equipped with telescopic sights. The Palestinians don't deny that they have these sights, and their official stance is that the individual weapon owners have purchased them. However, the IDF should consider that these might be specialist heavy-barrel weapons – possibly variants of the military gun used by civilians for hunting – which are being smuggled in from abroad, where they are legal and available in large numbers; even in the UK, it's perfectly legal to own such a weapon, as long as it has only a manually operated bolt. While the Palestinians' weapons are not dedicated sniper rifles, the addition of a good scope and a little training would greatly increase the capability of Palestinian long-range shooting. After all, the Washington Sniper, John Allen Muhammad, used a civilian M16 variant with a sniper scope, all bought commercially (see chapter ten).

This kind of retrofitting is a cheap way of obtaining high-quality rifles at a fraction of the cost of purpose-built sniper rifles. Weapons such as the AR15 H-Bar – a civilian semi-automatic-only version of the M16 – offer a high degree of accuracy – certainly out to 500m, at least. Meanwhile, there's enough information in literature and on the internet that would enable anyone to learn the basics of sniping and long-range shooting. There will never be a substitute for practice and professional training, but, if the aim is to deliver a round at an unsuspecting soldier over a long distance, it can be done easily enough.

When looking at how snipers have become involved in the Occupied Territories, it's almost the complete opposite of the battle in Stalingrad. The key players on either side of the Russian battle were professionals: one a master sniper, the other a hunter, both of whom knew the science of a bullet in flight. In Hebron and other war-torn areas of the Territories, amateurs appear to be fighting amateurs, each through scopes, with an unsettling dose of professional mercenaries thrown into the pot to confuse the situation further.

It's a highly regrettable fact that sniping in Gaza and the West Bank has become associated with one of two news stories: either that an innocent child has somehow been mistaken for a Palestinian sniper with an AK47, or that yet another brave IDF soldier has been cruelly cut down by a terrorist. Finding the truth about sniping in the West Bank is actually very difficult, as the more deeply you dig into each shooting, the more the truth is hidden, and the story invariably splits into two very different and predictable accounts.

Snipers are tools to be deployed as military tacticians see fit. There is truth in the theory that the IDF has used snipers as assassins, but this, be it right or wrong, is actually more akin to the true thrust of the sniper on the battlefield: a single shot at a high-value target. However, it's the many stories of military snipers who kill civilians that dominate the news concerning snipers in the Territories. It's unlikely that most of these shots come from true military snipers. As with the Washington Sniper, the concept of the sniper strikes fear into the heart of the enemy, but, when both sides are so blinded by hatred, can we really believe anything we read?

A particularly distressing 'sniper' case involves the killing of a twelve-year-old Palestinian boy caught by small-arms fire. Walking in an open street when shooting broke out, both he and his father sought cover, out of sight of the Israeli checkpoint, where most bystanders assumed the shooting was coming from, or being directed to. As the boy was sheltering behind an abandoned oil drum, shots from another direction killed him, while his father was badly wounded. Initially, the soldiers in the checkpoint were blamed for firing randomly, but an analysis of the shooting caught by a Palestinian TV crew showed that the bullet holes in the wall behind the body of the boy clearly indicated that the incoming rounds had been fired from another direction. And here the story splits.

The Palestinian view was that the shooting of the boy was proof of a ruthless Israeli sniping policy, regarding any target – civilian or paramilitary – as legitimate. Either that or it was the work of a contract sniper – possibly a Russian – who had been hired to kill Palestinians. There was an outcry, and the child's death added fuel to an already horrific conflict.

The Israelis have maintained to this day that they had no sniper operating in the area, and that the child's shooting had actually been orchestrated by the Palestinians in order to bring international condemnation on Israel. The boy had been sacrificed by his people, for his people. And this is possibly not so far-fetched a concept taken in the cultural context of martyrdom. It's possible that this young boy may have been one of the world's first sniper martyrs.

CHAPTER TWELVE

A Conversation with a Sniper

The one thing this book needed in order to be bang up to date and cutting edge was an interview with an active sniper. In this chapter, the identity of the sniper in question and the criteria of the interview have been obscured. This might appear to be a slightly melodramatic over-reaction, but, as the interviewee is still active and working in a 'peacekeeping' theatre, it is our decision – and our decision alone – to protect his identity.

The questions are presented simply and in the order they were presented.

What's the most difficult shot you've pulled off?

The driver of an armed pick-up truck moving over rough ground at 670m. Side profile of head and shoulders visible. One shot through the temple.

How do you prepare for a shot?

You can never prepare enough, but that shouldn't stop you trying. The most important things are that you get the variables right, such as range, wind, barometric pressure and survivability once the shot has been taken. The most important thing is that you prepare for the entire operation.

Why a sniper?

Because for me it was the ultimate professional challenge. Sniping is about taking basic infantry skills to a specialist level. The standards are very high, and there's a lot of self-reliance; if you make an error, you only have yourself to blame.

How do you feel about solitude? Do you ever feel cut off from the rest of the unit?

The days of operating as a lone wolf around the battlefield are pretty much over. Although we do operate forward of our own troops, we're always under the umbrella of indirect fire and try, where possible, to employ mutual support within pairs. That said, we do have to deal with some solitude, and potential snipers' suitability for this type of pressure is tested during the selection process.

What are the worst environmental conditions in which to shoot? What have been the worst conditions for you?

For me, operating in the desert during frequent sandstorms. The optics were useless. If you can't observe – a secondary role that you carry out 99 per cent of the time – then there's no point in being there.

Which snipers do you admire professionally? Why?

I've met and worked with many snipers I admire. However, I would have to say it would be someone I've never met: Major

Hesketh-Pritchard, author of *Sniping in France* and founder of British Army sniper training during the Great War on the eastern front. His techniques are still taught today. [11]

Do you see targets or people?
Targets, definitely. Although they do appear as people some time later.

What's your favoured weapon, and why?
The Accuracy International .338, due to its stand-off capability and consistency when used with Lapua ammunition. Also, the weight trade-off is negligible in comparison to its characteristics.

If you were denied access to a modern sniper rifle or gun and were restricted to arms made between 1900 and 1950, what would you carry?
A German Second World War Mauser rifle. They were years ahead in weapon and optical-sight design.

Have you ever faced another sniper?
No, but I've faced a number of sharpshooters. The difference is the use of fieldcraft.

Have you ever felt in mortal danger, perhaps from a sniper?
While withdrawing from an OP [Observation Point], my four-man team was ambushed by an enemy patrol. We had to fight our

11. While in this book we hope we have provided a new, plausible slant on some old themes – such as the deaths of Lord Nelson and John F Kennedy – we chose not to include previously published data. We acknowledge and accept Major Hesketh-Pritchard's work as an important document concerning sniping in the Great War, so anyone who wishes to learn more about this aspect of sniping should read the Major's book.

way out. Two of the snipers were using bolt-action rifles at extreme close quarters, which at some stages was hand-to-hand. We managed to extract, but we had one serious casualty. Four of the enemy had been killed. Snipers are supposed to stay on the fringes of the battle, use their long-range capability to observe and fire into it, not get in the middle. But that's one of the main risks with the 360-degree battlefield. Now I always carry my assault rifle as well as my sniper weapon.

What's your one golden rule?
Never flap.

What do your family know about your sniping excursions?
Nothing. It's the best way.

On retirement, what will be your most vivid memories of being a sniper?
The specialisation of the job and what an influence one well-trained sniper pair can have on a battle or operation.

How do you prepare for a trip?
As I said, you can never prepare too much. Failing to prepare is preparing to fail. I always try to get as much background on location as possible, then prep the kit, test the weapons and get in plenty of trigger time.

How do you relax after a trip?
Conduct a detailed debrief and then disengage for a couple of days.

Tell us about your training and practising. Is it conducted outside the country?
Initial training is normally carried out in the UK. Continuation

training takes place worldwide in all theatres: Arctic, desert, jungle, temperate, northwest Europe.

What great sniper shots in history intrigue you, and why?
The assassination of JFK – the head shot at a moving vehicle.

What assignment would you most like to undertake?
Professionally, I would have to say sniper on sniper.

What are your opinions on the Middle East?
Once you've experienced the place, you know that it's right that we're there.

Outside military life, what are your ambitions?
Long life and happiness. And to see Norwich City win the FA Cup.

What about inside military life?
To continue to have an impact on the way we train and employ our snipers.

What advice would you give a teenager hoping to be a sniper?
Take your time. Learn to be a good infantry soldier first. It takes a certain kind of maturity to be a good sniper.

Which country produces the best snipers?
Difficult question. In my opinion, the USA produces better shooters, but we produce the best at fieldcraft. The Kiwis are also very good.

Can you give us a real-life sniper story?

While operating in a particular country where it's very hot, [our sniper section] located an enemy compound, mounted 360-degree covert observation for twelve hours, then conducted a co-ordinated shoot from three OP locations. The enemy didn't have a clue and didn't even return any rounds. Within five minutes of the opening volley of shots, fourteen enemy were dead. The remaining six later surrendered to friendly forces. We extracted unseen.

EPILOGUE

The Media Machine

The media are a mass of contradiction, and somewhere in the middle lies the truth. Newspaper journalists and editors build up pop and sports stars, only to bring them down – certainly in Britain. They also fight amongst themselves over the intricate facts concerning covert police operations in order to gain the exclusive, justifying such squabbling as a legitimate search for facts that, they feel, the public have a right to know.

This part of the book isn't intended to be an essay about the moral stance of the media; too many good observations have been made so far in this book, so we don't dwell on the subject. Interestingly, though, Montgomery County Police Chief Charles Moose explained how the media had acted as both saint and sinner during the Washington Sniper incident. The press are rarely the good guys all the time, but then, it's their job to push the facts.

With the Washington Sniper incident, the media finally got a story with a beginning, a middle and an end, but what happens when the story doesn't have a happy ending? What about the John

F Kennedy shooting? No matter what your personal beliefs are about Kennedy's assassination – whether or not Oswald did it – you can't get away from the fact that more was going on during that day in Dallas than is publicly acknowledged. And, with any intrigue, there's a big news story; and with big news stories, there's always a big book deal; and with a big book deal, there's a big movie; and, somewhere along the line, the truth gets lost.

As far as Kennedy is concerned, the best screen interpretations are *Kennedy*, starring Martin Sheen, and of course Oliver Stone's *JFK*. But are these movies true to historical fact? Probably not, because we don't know what the historical fact actually is. The jigsaw is incomplete, the final verdict open to interpretation. And the intrigue goes on...

Let's look at another movie: *Dirty Harry*. Apart from being one of Clint Eastwood's greatest movies, this film is the epitome of the American-psycho-with-a-scope scenario. Scorpio – the bad-guy sniper – kills for money but justifies his actions through his political and social rantings, which are those of a true madman (he can't see that what he does is wrong and feels persecuted by Clint Eastwood's good-guy cop, Harry Callahan). But all that doesn't touch on the ultimate irony of the movie: yes, Andy Robinson gives an incredibly strong performance as Scorpio, but it's what the media brought to the movie that's important. The character of 'Dirty' Harry was labelled a fascist, the film lambasted for portraying right-wing ideologies, but that wasn't the point at all.

Take a look at the scene that opens the movie, covering the tombstone inscribed with the names of the San Francisco Police Department who lost their lives fighting for justice. Harry is disillusioned at the predicament he finds himself in, tied up by bureaucratic red tape. He is weary of the police force of which he is an integral part. He has lost good partners, good friends. He doesn't believe in vigilantes (as is later made clear in the film's sequel, *Magnum Force*). The sniper in the movie is both bad guy and partial victim.

As mentioned in the Authors' Note to this book, a work concerning snipers raises an important question concerning snipers: does their continued presence – for good or bad – and the fact that we feel the need to write about them indicate that there's something wrong with our society, just as it must be morally wrong to sympathise with Charles Bronson's 'hero' in the first *Death Wish* movie? *Dirty Harry* is immersed in that media contradiction; it takes up the issues and isn't afraid to discuss them, and that's what makes it the best sniper movie ever made. The fact that the sniper is putting together his gun on a roof with a helicopter behind him – and he doesn't even notice! – is neither here nor there. In a way, the hectic amateurism of the psycho correlates with the arguments that the Washington Sniper wasn't really a sniper, just a nutter with a gun who must be classified as a sniper for reasons of clarity.

Let's look at government and military snipers for a moment. It would be great to see a TV movie based on the James Bond short story *The Living Daylights* (it's highly unlikely that there would ever be a loyal cinema interpretation!). The whole story concerns the mentality of two snipers, and author Ian Fleming shows his own keen perception of such quasi-military skill, getting much further under the skin of the lone sniper than anyone had ever done before the story was written, in the mid-1960s. It's a truly breathtaking read.

In juxtaposition to the Kennedy assassination is the non-assassination of General Charles de Gaulle, President of France. The Organisation de l'Armée Secrète (OAS) tried many times to kill the President but failed. It took Frederick Forsyth – a Reuters reporter based in Paris – to wonder, 'Why don't they hire a hit man?' The resulting novel, *The Day of the Jackal*, succeeds because the assassin doesn't. We all know that de Gaulle wasn't assassinated, but the story's strength lies in the 'real-life' scenario created by Forsyth and the air of mystery he created. We don't truly know who the jackal is – his name, his history or anything else – and this makes him one of the most dangerous types of sniper. But maybe that's what makes him typical of all snipers; when his cover is blown, the sniper must escape.

Some movie adaptations have chilling conclusions that weren't present in the original novel. A good example of this is the famous Statue of Liberty scene that concludes the original *Planet of the Apes* movie, which didn't feature in Pierre Boulle's 1963 book. Another, more relevant example is the conclusion of the Michael Caine classic *Get Carter*. At the end of Ted Lewis's novel – titled *Jack's Return Home*, which is actually narrated by the main character – Jack has been shot but isn't dead, whereas in the movie an unknown sniper is called in and calmly, coldly takes out Carter on a windy beach and goes home rather casually afterwards.

Perhaps the interpretation of the sniper in *Get Carter* is more realistic than that of any other movie, even though his presence takes up only a few feet of celluloid. Here we have the successful professional sniper. He is paid. He carries out his job quickly and efficiently, and then returns to his own world. The only problem is with the sniper shot itself. It's impossible, not because of the wind factor on the beach (a good sniper could have dealt with that) but because of the way Caine moves his head just as the shot is fired. The action is so sharp and unnatural that the sniper would surely miss, as it occurs at the same second as the shot. That said, it's still a great movie!

There is also great sniper action in the movie *Enemy at the Gates*, but not of the same measure as that in David L Robbins's novel *War of the Rats*, on which the movie was based. Robbins' novel portrays the same 'faction' that appear in Forsyth's *The Day of the Jackal*, taking a truth and wrapping a fiction around it, thus enabling the reader to complete the jigsaw. The end of this film also features a highly suspect sniper shoot that's nothing like the professional stand-off so chillingly described in the original novel.

Truth with a heretofore untold angle; fiction based upon a logical outcome; the reality of war and covert operations – big news stories, all describing the anatomy of the media machine that lives off suffering.

The human race is a destructive beast that's fascinated by its own power to destroy, hiding mysteries seductively behind the broad excuses it creates to justify its own existence. It's up to each person to decide whether those excuses are ultimately for good or ill. Ask 1,000 people and expect 1,000 different answers. As far as the sniper is concerned, he is here to stay. As long as the bad guys keep coming at us, we need the sniper on-side and the bad guy in-scope.

Craig Cabell
London, July 2005

ANNEXE A

Sniper Rifles and Ammunition

Someone in the motorcar trade once said, 'No one actually builds a bad car today. Some are just better than others.' The same observation can be made about the sniper's main tool: his rifle. There are innumerable highly accurate rifles on the market today, most of which are produced for the hunting market. On pure straight-line accuracy and power, these guns are perfectly adequate for most long-range shooting, but they've not been designed for 'military use' – a well-known euphemism for 'harsh treatment in all environments by people who won't necessarily look after their equipment as well as the manufacturer might like'.

Those of us who shoot most likely own perfectly well-built, possibly even semi-ruggedised weapons, but would they stand up to conditions in the battlefield? Certainly not. Our scopes definitely wouldn't.

For a rifle to be considered worthy of being classed as a sniper rifle, it must meet two basic criteria: it must be able to operate in all weather conditions and it must be supremely accurate. All sniper rifles can do this. Some just do it better than others.

So, by this rationale, should we assume that a sniper is only as good as his gun? Of course not. As we've explored in this book, all good snipers share an inherent skill in tracking and hunting their target. A good tool just gives them the edge. Good shooting is in the blood. You either have the skill or you don't. Your talent as a sniper might be due to your ability to control your breathing or stay calm, or perhaps the strength of vision in one of your eyes – biological issues that cannot be improved with training. The fact is that tactical snipers can be manufactured, while good shooters cannot. They are born with the necessary skills already in place.

Of course, a good gun will make the sniper's job easier, in the same way that using a cordless electric drill rather than a hand drill makes a carpenter's job easier. But it doesn't make the carpenter any more talented; it just gives him one less thing to worry about. The sniper can wake on a cold winter's morning and take up a dawn position with the sun behind him and not worry that his rifle, which was exposed all night, has a frozen bolt. He knows his rifle is designed to operate in all conditions. This reliability promotes confidence in the shooter.

To illustrate this confidence I trust the reader will indulge a personal experience from one of the authors; Richard Brown:

During the writing of this book, I was lucky enough to have the opportunity to fire several 7.62mm sniper rifles on a good range. The weapons were both bolt-action and semi-automatic, although for various reasons I won't divulge the specific models. Suffice to say that they were all of an exceptionally high quality and were equipped with superior scopes.

I began by shooting at a distance of 600m. This was the

longest range I had shot at, and I have no hesitation in saying that the targets seem impossibly small at this range, which was far in excess of those I'd shot at previously, and I initially found the prospect rather daunting. Nevertheless, I was confident that, after the research both Craig and I had done for this book, the rifles would be perfectly accurate at such a range.

Lying prone, with my eye pressed to the scope, I felt this same confidence – not due to the small ability I have as a shooter but, primarily, due to knowing that I had the finest equipment of its genre nestled against my body. The rounds looked suitably lethal as I slipped them one by one into the magazine, and there was a particularly reassuring slap as I cocked and chambered the semi-automatic weapon.

I was very familiar with the model of rifle I was using and well aware of the expected trigger pull, and the gun performed exactly as I'd envisaged. There was a fearsome boom as the round discharged and the rifle moved up and backwards, the bipod momentarily appearing to lift from the ground. Immediately, I knew that the round had hit home, and for the first time I truly appreciated just how accurate such a gun is at long ranges. Even though we were firing at 600m – one hell of distance to someone who is historically a handgunner! – I realised that the gun would be just as accurate at 1,000m. I have shot sniper rifles many times before, but not since Craig and I had begun to study both the weapons and their place in the world of firearms.

The second shot was as smooth as the first, and already I was used to the noise and recoil. Before long, the magazine was empty and there was a neat 6-inch group of holes in the target, over half a kilometre away. Several magazines later, I felt very much at home with the rifle and was itching to push out the range.

Shortly after the session with the semi-automatic, I had a go with a number of modern bolt-action rifles. Again, I'd fired bolt-actions before – indeed, I'd fired one particular model of weapon just a few months earlier – but this proved a wonderful chance to fire rifles with both types of operating mechanism in one day. While I personally prefer semi-automatic guns, there's something very satisfying about operating a bolt-action rifle. There is a real visual and physical sense of loading each round, of seeing it fed gently into the chamber, of pulling the bolt back and releasing smoke and a steaming hot case. Seeing the open-necked case come out of the gun and land next to you really drives home the sensation that you've actually delivered the round. (It was interesting to note that the semi-auto kicked the cases so far away, and at such speed, that we never found all of them.)

In my opinion, bolt-action rifles have the potential to breed a better shooter, because you don't have that immediate second round, and so you need to concentrate just a little more on each shot. Although the cycling of the mechanism was swift and smooth, the gun I was using was slower than the self-loader and I broke the golden rule I was taught as a very young shooter and changed my grip.

Nevertheless, the session was an excellent experience and only served to reaffirm my full admiration for the manufacturers who produce these perfect weapons around the world and men and woman who spend their lives being at one with them.

One of the bolt-action guns had been zeroed with a particular breed of ammunition, and this leads conveniently on to the next element of sniper equipment.

Poor ammunition will seriously hinder a sniper's capabilities, as it will any shooter. By using substandard ammunition, you'll be leaving yourself open to inconsistent velocity, fouling, excessive smoke (especially dangerous for a sniper) and poor feeding. If you're ever given the opportunity, have a go at shooting a gun first with poor ammunition and then with high-quality rounds. The difference is quite noticeable, and it becomes more of an issue as the distance between you and the target increases. Small perambulations a few centimetres from the muzzle will become 2m near misses at 500m.

In order for a gun to be genuinely described as being a sniper rifle, it must be capable of delivering highly accurately rounds over long ranges. If the sniper is to become one with the rifle and 'feel' where the rounds are going, he needs to be able to anticipate the performance of each round in flight, and he can only do this if the performance of one round is identical to the next. After all, the whole process involves the shooter sending a tiny piece of lead out of the machine. This sounds a pretty fundamental point, but when you stand a bullet (without its case) next to a rifle, the difference in weight between such a tiny object and the machine that's designed to fire it seems vast.

Sniper ammunition – or 'Match ammunition', as it's often called – is big business. With any gun – pistol, rifle or sub-machine gun – your shooting will be fundamentally affected by whichever ammunition you choose to use. The poorer its quality, the less accurate the weapon will be. A good example of this – albeit in a handgun – can be seen in the following brief account from a fellow shooter, following a day of plinking on a range:

> Back in 1996, when target pistols could still be legally held in the UK, our gun club took possession of a cheap batch of around 5,000 .22 LR Yugoslav-manufacture rounds. Even

before shooting the bullets, it was apparent that the ammunition was poor quality. The rounds were rough to touch and the brass was mottled. The lead heads were the same size but there were small chips and marks on each round, indicating that little care had been taken to achieve any consistency of manufacture. At the time, I resisted the temptation to fire the ammunition from a quality self-loading target pistol such as a Hammerli and opted for a more forgiving .22 LR Walther PPK. The rounds boasted to be high-velocity, so there should have been little trouble with cycling the PPK's heavier slide.

Accuracy was at best poor at 10m, and the smell was truly awful! After three magazines, the PPK began to foul badly as residue dropped into the magazine. Soon the magazine began to jam, the feed plates sticking at the lips of the magazine and failing to load the next round. I eventually resorted to 'cooking' the ammunition off in a 6-inch Smith & Wesson Model 17-5 revolver, which had a club reputation for chewing anything that happened to be the right calibre. At least it couldn't jam in that gun, but it was damned hard to eject the cases after six rounds had been fired. They expanded like any other case will do, but they never went back to anything close to their original size, so they wedged in the chambers. It was a good lesson: your shooting is only as good as your ammo. You load crap into the gun and most likely that's what will come out.

'Plinking Sessions' with poor-quality ammunition can be fun, because there's not much more you can do with it – although, of course, you'll spend the next hour cleaning your gun. If your life depends on the ammunition performing properly, however, the matter suddenly becomes a lot more serious. It's for this reason that the UK armed forces impose strict criteria for the selection of not only sniper rifles but also of the ammunition used with it. When you've invested upwards of £5,000 on a sniper rifle for a well-trained operative and vast sums on training, it's a false economy to settle for anything but the very best in ammunition.

During our research for this book, we came across a documentary account of the level of assessment armed forces put into the selection of a new round. Below are extracts from a document written by Colonel W Hays Park of the USMC in 1985, when the USMC were debating whether they could, or should, begin deploying open-tip (more commonly known as 'hollow-point') ammunition. It's clear from the text that the colonel is of the opinion that the ammunition is of a high quality and should be deployed. However, there is an issue to overcome: that of using expanding ammunition in a theatre of war:

Background

Sierra MatchKing 168-Grain Match-Grade Boat-Tail

For more than a decade, two bullets have been available for use by the United States Army Marksmanship Unit in match competition in its 7.62mm rifles. The M118 is a 173-grain match-grade, full-metal-jacket boat-tail, ogival spitzer-tip bullet, while the M852 is the Sierra MatchKing 168-grain match-grade boat-tail, ogival spitzer-tip bullet with an open tip. Although the accuracy of the M118 has been reasonably good, though at times erratic, independent bullet comparisons by the Army, Marine Corps and National Guard marksmanship training units have established unequivocally the superior accuracy of the M852. Army tests noted a 36 per cent improvement in accuracy with the M852 at 300m, and a 32 per cent improvement at 600 yards; Marine Corps figures were 28 per cent accuracy improvement at 300m and

20 per cent at 600 yards. The National Guard determined that the M852 provided better bullet groups at 200 and 600 yards under all conditions than did the M118.

The 168-grain MatchKing was designed in the late 1950s for 300m shooting in international rifle matches. In its competitive debut, it was used by the first-place winner at the 1959 Pan-American Games. In the same calibre, but in its various bullet lengths, the MatchKing has set a number of international records. To a range of 600m, the superiority of the accuracy of the M852 cannot be matched and led to the decision by US military marksmanship training units to use the M852 in competition.

A 1980 opinion of this office concluded that use of the M852 in match competition would not violate law-of-war obligations of the United States... Further tests and actual competition over the past decade have confirmed the superiority of the M852 over the M118 and other match-grade bullets. For example, at the national matches held at Camp Perry, Ohio, in 1983, a new Wimbledon record of 2,015 Xs was set using the 168-grain MatchKing. This level of performance led to the question of whether the M852 could be used by military snipers in peacetime or wartime missions of the Army.

During the period in which this review was conducted, the 180-grain MatchKing [for which there is no military designation] also was tested with a view to increased accuracy over the M852 at very long ranges. Because two bullet weights were under consideration, the term 'MatchKing' will be used hereinafter to refer to the generic design rather than to a bullet of a particular weight. The fundamental question to be addressed by this review is whether an open-tip bullet of MatchKing design may be used in combat.

Here, two Match-grade rounds are being compared. Match ammunition has always been of the highest quality, but ballistic technology moves on, just as it does with every other machine. A round designed in the 1950s rarely compares in ballistic performance to a relatively new round. What was once considered a 'man-stopper' can become obsolete in the space of thirty years. Already, common rounds such as the .45 ACP and the ubiquitous 9mm x19 are being easily outclassed by super-fast and small bullets such as the 5.7mm and 4.6mm rounds fired from the FN Herstal P90 and the Heckler & Koch MP7 PDW, respectively, which can penetrate body armour at 200m and still have sufficient energy to leave terrible wounds in the target. At 25m, a 9mm round cannot even penetrate a standard-issue NATO military helmet.

Going back to Colonel Hays Parks's dilemma at the USMC, the Colonel took the time to look at the legal ramifications involved with using hollow-point ammunition:

Legal Factors

The principal provision relating to the legality of weapons is contained in Art. 23e of the *Annex to Hague Convention IV: Respecting the Laws and Customs of War on Land* of 18 October 1907, which prohibits the employment of 'arms, projectiles or material of a nature to cause superfluous injury'. In some law-of-war treatises, the term 'unnecessary suffering' is used rather than 'superfluous injury'. The terms are regarded as synonymous. To emphasise this, Art. 35, para. 2 of the 1977 Protocol I Additional to the Geneva Conventions of 12 August 1949 states in part that 'It is prohibited to employ weapons [and] projectiles... of a nature to cause superfluous injury or unnecessary suffering.' Although the US has made the formal decision that for military, political, and humanitarian reasons it will not become a party to Protocol I, US officials have taken the position that the language of Art. 35(2) of Protocol I, as quoted, is a codification of customary international law and therefore binding upon all nations. The terms 'unnecessary suffering' and 'superfluous injury' have not been formally defined within international law.

In determining whether a weapon or projectile causes unnecessary suffering, a balancing test is applied between the force dictated by military necessity to achieve a legitimate objective vis à vis suffering that may be considered superfluous to achievement of that intended objective. The test is not easily applied. For this reason, the degree of 'superfluous' injury must be clearly disproportionate to the intended objectives for the development and employment of the weapon – that is, it must outweigh substantially the military necessity for the weapon system or projectile. The fact that a weapon causes suffering does not lead to the conclusion that the weapon causes unnecessary suffering or is illegal *per se*. Military necessity dictates that weapons of war lead to death, injury and destruction; the act of combatants killing or wounding enemy combatants in combat is a legitimate act under the law of war. In this regard, there is an incongruity in the law of war in that, while it is legally permissible to kill an enemy combatant, incapacitation must not result inevitably in unnecessary suffering. What is prohibited is the design (or modification) and employment of a weapon for the purpose of increasing or causing suffering beyond that required by military necessity.

In conducting the balancing test necessary to determine a weapon's legality, the effects of a weapon cannot be viewed in isolation. They must be examined against comparable weapons in use on the modern battlefield, and the military necessity for the weapon or projectile [must be considered].

In addition to the basic prohibition on unnecessary suffering contained in Art. 23e of the 1907 Hague IV, one other treaty is germane to this review. The *Hague Declaration Concerning Expanding Bullets* of 29 July 1899 prohibits the use in international armed conflict '... of bullets which expand or flatten easily in the human body, such as bullets with a hard envelope which does not entirely cover the core or is pierced with incisions.' The US is not a party to this treaty, but US officials over the years have taken the position that the armed forces of the US will adhere to its terms to the extent that its application is consistent with the object and purpose of Art. 23e of the Annex to the Hague Convention IV, quoted above.

It is within the context of these two treaties that questions regarding the legality of the employment of the MatchKing open-tip bullet must be considered.

Cutting through the legalese shown above, the Colonel here is analysing whether the hollow-point sniper round is simply too destructive to be used against a human being. More often than you might imagine, weapons are developed that are considered too injurious for actual use in combat. The deployment of such weapons would cause so much suffering that they are banned under an Article within the Hague Convention of 1907.

Probably the most famous example of ammunition considered too damaging to use is the dum-dum bullet. This small-arms round was first developed by the British Army for use in India, in less politically correct times, at the Dum-Dum Arsenal near Calcutta in the late 1890s. It comprised a jacketed .303 bullet, with the jacket nose open to expose its lead core. The aim was to improve the bullet's effectiveness by increasing its expansion upon impact.

Expanding bullets are now fairly common, but their use and manufacture are controlled, and still there are some rounds that attract legal attention. Many modern hunting rounds split into several shards on impact, creating multiple wound channels, and their use is not permitted in war. Equally, soldiers found altering rounds, such as by cutting a cross into the lead tip, face severe consequences.

In Colonel Hays Parks's report for the USMC, he then describes the controversial bullet that he intends to issue to snipers and assesses its performance:

Bullet Description

As previously described, the MatchKing is a boat-tail, ogival spitzer-tip bullet with open tip. The 'open tip' is a shallow aperture (approximately the diameter of the wire in a standard-size straight pin or paper clip) in the nose of the bullet. While sometimes described as a 'hollow point', this is a mischaracterisation in law-of-war terms. Generally, a 'hollow-point' bullet is thought of in terms of its ability to expand on impact with soft tissue. Physical examination of the MatchKing 'open-tip' bullet reveals that its opening is extremely small in comparison to the aperture in comparable hollow-point hunting bullets; for example, the 165-grain GameKing is a true hollow-point boat-tail bullet, with an aperture substantially greater than the MatchKing and skiving [serrations cut into the jacket] to ensure expansion.

In the MatchKing, the open tip is closed as much as possible to provide better aerodynamics, and contains no skiving. The lead core of the MatchKing bullet is entirely covered by the bullet jacket. While the GameKing bullet is designed to bring the ballistic advantages of a match bullet to long-range hunting, the manufacturer expressly recommends against the use of the MatchKing for hunting game of any size because [the round] does not have the expansion characteristics of a hunting bullet.

The purpose of the small, shallow aperture in the MatchKing is to provide a bullet design offering maximum accuracy at very long ranges, rolling the jacket of the bullet around its core from base to tip; standard military bullets and other Match bullets roll the jacket around its core from tip to base, leaving an exposed lead core at its base. The design purpose of the MatchKing was not to produce a bullet that would expand or flatten easily on impact with the human body, or otherwise cause wounds greater than those caused by standard military small-arms ammunition.

MatchKing Performance

Other than its superior long-range-marksmanship capabilities, the MatchKing was examined with regard to its performance on impact with the human body or in artificial material that approximates human soft tissue. It was determined that the bullet will break up or fragment in some cases at some point following entry into soft tissue. Whether fragmentation occurs will depend upon a myriad of variables, to include range to the target, velocity at the time of impact, degree of yaw of the bullet at the point of impact [and] the distance travelled point-first within the body before yaw is induced. The MatchKing has not been designed intentionally to yaw or to break up on impact; these characteristics are common to all military rifle bullets. There was little discernible difference in bullet fragmentation between the

MatchKing and other military small-arms bullets, with some military ball ammunition of foreign manufacture tending to fragment sooner in human tissue or to a greater degree, resulting in wounds that would be more severe than those caused by the MatchKing.

Because of concern over the potential mischaracterisation of the M852 as a 'hollow-point' bullet, which might violate the purpose and intent of the 1899 *Hague Declaration Concerning Expanding Bullets*, some M852 MatchKing bullets were modified to close the aperture. The 'closed-tip' MatchKing did not measure up to the accuracy of the 'open-tip' MatchKing.

Other Match grade bullets were tested. While some could approach the accuracy standards of the MatchKing in some lots, quality control was uneven, leading to erratic results. No other Match-grade bullet consistently could meet the accuracy of the open-tip bullet.'

Obviously keen to support his own case, the Colonel summarises and concludes:

In World War II, the United States and its allies expended 25,000 rounds of ammunition to kill a single enemy soldier. In the Korean War, the ammunition expenditure had increased four-fold to 100,000 rounds per soldier. In the Vietnam War, that figure had doubled to 200,000 rounds of ammunition for the death of a single enemy soldier. The risk to non-combatants is apparent.

In contrast, United States Army and Marine Corps snipers in the Vietnam War expended 1.3 rounds of ammunition for each claimed and verified kill, at an average range of 600 yards, or almost twice the 300m cited above for combat engagements by the average soldier. Some verified kills were at ranges in excess of 1,000 yards. This represents discrimination and military efficiency of the highest order, as well as minimisation of risk to non-combatants. Utilisation of a bullet that increases accuracy, such as the MatchKing, would further diminish the risk to non-combatants.

Conclusion

The purpose of the 7.62mm 'open-tip' MatchKing bullet is to provide maximum accuracy at very long range. Like most 5.56mm and 7.62mm military ball bullets, it may fragment upon striking its target, although the probability of its fragmentation is not as great as some military ball bullets currently in use by some nations. Bullet fragmentation is not a design characteristic, however, nor a purpose for use of the MatchKing by United States Army snipers. Wounds caused by MatchKing ammunition are similar to those caused by a fully jacketed military ball bullet – which is legal under the law of war – when compared at the same ranges and under the same conditions. The military necessity for its use – its ability to offer maximum accuracy at very long ranges – is complemented by the high degree of discriminate fire it offers in the hands of a trained sniper. It not only meets but also exceeds the law-of-war obligations of the United States for use in combat.

The above case is a good example of the length that the armed forces will go to in order to ensure that their snipers have the very best rounds for their rifles. It illustrates perfectly the point we've been making: you need the very best ammunition for a sniper rifle, and if there's a potential problem with it then you find a way around it.

Today, the most common sniper rounds, in no particular order, are:

7.62MM X 51 OR .308 WINCHESTER. (Here, the '7.62mm' refers to the calibre of the gun, while and the 'x51' refers to the length of the cartridge case in millimetres.) This bullet is actually bigger than 7.62mm – in fact, it's around 7.82mm – so that it is gripped completely by the rifling of the barrel and creates a perfect gas seal ahead of the charge.

The 7.62mm (.308) enjoys success in both military and civilian fields. It's an excellent hunting round and has been adopted by NATO as their standard sniping bullet. Although today's small-arms manufacturers still make most of their weapons in 7.62mm, there are some schools of thought that suggest that this calibre, which has been the backbone of sniping for countless years, is now old and outdated. As ballistic protection is developed for both humans and vehicles, the 7.62mm round is relatively easily defeated. It will no doubt continue to be popular as a hunting round, but as a military round its days are almost certainly numbered.

Typically, a 7.62mm round has a bullet weight of around 150–168 grains (9–10g), a muzzle velocity of 2,700fps (820mps) and muzzle energy of 3,500J (approximately 2,600ft/lb).

.338 (8.59MM). This round has become increasingly popular over the last few years, bridging the gap between the ageing 7.62mm and the larger, anti-material rounds, such as .50 calibre. It's a noticeably larger round than the former and has an impressive ballistic performance. It fires on a very flat trajectory and carries substantial foot poundage (ft/lb) at long ranges. At 1,000m, it still delivers well in excess of 1, 200ft/lb of energy. (When you consider that the average 9mm delivers

250–300ft/lbs on leaving the muzzle of the gun, the statistics become more impressive.)

Typically a .338 round has a bullet weight of around 250 grains (16g), a muzzle velocity of 3,000fps (915mps) and muzzle energy of 6,782J (approximately 5,000ft/lb).

.50 BMG. This is a massive round with awesome capabilities in a sniper rifle. The 'BMG' designation following the calibre stands for 'Browning Machine Gun' (although other, more graphic definitions have been suggested!). Typically a .50 BMG round has a bullet weight of around 700 grains (45g), a muzzle velocity of 2,900fps (880mps) and muzzle energy of 16,990J (approximately 12,500ft/lb).

Deployed against humans, this is a devastating piece of ammunition. A rifle in this calibre – a Barrett Model 82A1 – has the dubious honour of claiming the longest authenticated sniper kill in recent conflicts, when an Iraqi soldier was killed by a US sniper team at the impressive range of 1,800m during the liberation of Kuwait. It's also amazing to think that the .50 BMG round hit this target, at that range, with more force than a .44 Magnum would have at point-blank distance. (There is a persistent rumour that another target was eliminated in a recent war at 2,200m, but it has yet to be confirmed.)

The real benefit of the .50 BMG lies in its good anti-materiel capabilities. Shooting at non-human targets is becoming a more common part of the snipers' job description. With a rifle capable of delivering such force at long ranges, it's now possible for a single sniper to create havoc at airfields and other strategic bases. A .50 BMG round delivered to a crucial part of a stationary aircraft or helicopter will ground the machine permanently. Equally, there are weak points on armoured vehicles, such as night-vision units and periscopes, that can be taken out just as easily. Communications antennae and satellite dishes are also vulnerable to such a weapon. Smash the enemy's comms and he's cut off. And what engineer is going to volunteer to climb on to the roof to effect repairs when he knows that there's a sniper in the area?

Concluding this brief look at projectiles, we conveniently come full circle and take a look at the machines that deliver them. As we have briefly stated before, the first sniper rifles were no more than standard infantry rifles pulled from the production line if they showed above-average accuracy at the test-fire stage. They were then subjected to a process called 'accurising'. This process remained the norm until purpose-built sniper rifles began to appear in the 1980s.

In order to be considered a sniper rifle, a gun must have some basic features. It must be able to take a scope, for instance, and be comfortable enough for a shooter to hold for many hours. Early sniper rifles were more accurate than their standard-issue brethren, often through luck – for instance, when a gun came off the production line, its rifling might have been given the optimum twist to give the round a higher speed than other guns in the batch.

Once it had been selected as a potential sniper weapon, the gun's mechanism would then be stripped and reworked by hand in order to be smooth and as silent as possible in its operation. On old weapons, such as the Lee-Enfield, a 'cheek piece' would simply be bolted on to the butt, allowing the shooter to get a perfect angle of vision through the scope – which at the time of its manufacture would have been basic, with a very narrow field of vision. We recently looked through a Second World War German scope, mounted on an accurised Mauser K98, and the difference between this old military specification sight and a relatively inexpensive civilian sight today is vast. One note of interest was that the German scope has a T-shaped reticle, as opposed to the more traditional cross, thus:

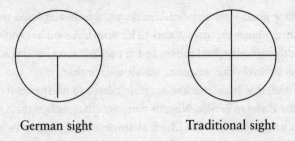

German sight   Traditional sight

The T-shaped reticle is considered by many snipers to be the best shape. A sniper spends a great deal of time looking though the scope and not actually shooting, and the T-shaped crosshairs leave the top half of the scope free for roaming and the join of the T can easily be brought to bear on the target. No matter where you look on the traditional crosshair scope, there's a line to distract your vision. It's a small point but one that causes much debate amongst shooters.

It was never the intention for this book to be a technical gun book – there are too many out there already – but we should take time here to look more closely at sniper rifles themselves. To this end, we've selected two guns to compare: a semi-automatic from the old Eastern Bloc and a Western bolt-action rifle – two very different guns with two very different operating methods which, in the dark days of the Cold War, would have been aimed at each other. They are the Russian Dragunov and the British L42A1.

During the Second World War, the British Army used accurised .303 Lee-Enfield No. 4 rifles, which were designated as sniper rifles by having a T added to the name. These guns differed very little from the standard infantry rifle but were super-accurate models that had been selected from production runs. To this standard gun, a bolt-on cheek piece was added in order to give the shooter a good view through the scope, which was fixed on to a rail fitted above the iron sights. The bolt lever on a Lee-Enfield faces downwards when at rest and is cocked upwards through 90 degrees to cycle the weapon, which meant that, when the scope was fitted, this basic mechanism didn't have to be altered – unlike with the Russian Mosin Nagant rifle. To change this into a sniper rifle, a new bolt had to be fitted, as the standard Nagant bolt rests horizontal to the gun and is cocked 90 degrees to face perpendicularly upwards to the gun, which obviously prevents the fitting of a scope. Therefore, the Nagant sniper rifle has a new bolt fitted to it, which is much like the Enfield's.

In the 1960s, it became clear to the British Army that they needed to develop a dedicated sniper rifle that utilised the new 7.62mm NATO round. Rather than embrace a new weapon, the military took the odd decision to look backwards at its firearm arsenal and revamp the ageing Lee-Enfield, transforming it into a new sniper rifle. This practice of retrofitting is actually quite common for UK military small arms; although some parties criticise the current 5.56mm SA80, we should actually consider ourselves fortunate that the British Army even *has* a modern gun.

In the Great War, the British Army carried the fine short-magazine Lee-Enfield .303 rifle. The Mk III rifle, which saw extensive service in between 1914 and 1918, was a complex weapon, but it was very well made and robust. Nevertheless, it boasted one particularly odd feature which harked back to the single-shot rifles of the 1800s. The British Army feared the consequences of soldiers having a ten-shot magazine – this would surely signify the end of well-aimed, accurate shooting – so, a cut-off plate was added that actually prevented the rounds from feeding upwards from the magazine. The soldier was encouraged to open the bolt and manually feed in a single round. Fortunately, this madness was stopped in the 1920s, when the Mk III* was introduced. This rifle had no such cut-off plate and its rear sight had been moved to the back of the gun, rather than the middle, making aiming much easier.

Even so, the British military's bizarre attitude to guns persisted into the time of the Second World War. When the US Army began to embrace the concept of semi-automatic weapons, Britain still insisted on issuing bolt-action guns, such as the No. 4 Lee-Enfield, the standard British rifle between 1939 and 1945. This was undeniably a superb gun, but with its bolt action it couldn't compete against its semi-automatic rivals. Unlike the Americans, with their M1 Garands, and the Germans, who were developing the MP44, British soldiers were very late in being exposed to the benefits of semi-automatic weapons.

And so it continued. In the 1970s and 1980s, the Russians grew accustomed to their fully automatic Kalashnikovs and the Americans to their similarly equipped M16s while the British Army still used the very heavy, and only semi-automatic, SLR. The British military was horribly late in accepting that the 5.56mm round was the future of military small arms. Indeed, right up to the Falklands conflict, British troops were still issued with the outdated SLR. During this conflict, there were cases of UK troops actually dumping their ageing SLRs and arming themselves with stolen Argentine 5.56mm fully automatic assault rifles. This meant that they could carry more ammunition – of which there was plenty lying around – and gave them the benefit of having a weapon with less recoil and more firepower. Finally, twenty years after the world had issued 5.56mm guns to most armies, the SA80 was brought into widespread service in the British military.

This, of course, was the situation that led to the development in the 1960s of the L42A1, which was based on the Lee-Enfield No. 4 design but altered to meet sniper requirements. To this end, it was re-barrelled to accommodate the NATO 7.62mm round, a rail was fitted so that a scope could be attached and a cheek piece was added to the butt. The rail and cheek support were no different to the additions to the Second World War No. 4 (T), but the barrel was different, although the scope was a modified version of the 1940s model. And there it was – the British Army had a new sniper weapon.

Adopting the characteristics of the original Lee-Enfield gun gave the L42A1 a good background. With the mechanism tuned to perfection, it was a superbly accurate weapon, and today the British Army use a similar bolt-action rifle of modern polymer design.

Dragunov

By comparison, the Russian Dragunov was radical when it first appeared. Elements of the gun resemble the Kalashnikov range, although the two are fundamentally different weapons.

Unlike the British, the Russians have always seen the value of snipers (see chapter six). As they upgraded their entire arsenal in preparation for the Cold War, they included their sniper rifle. In the 1960s, Western intelligence soon learned of the new gun and, on its capture, suspicions of a new super-sniper rifle were confirmed. The Dragunov outclassed anything the West was using, and even today it's still a formidable rifle, capable of one-shot kill in excess of 800m.

Unlike the UK's standard sniper rifle, the Dragunov (named after its creator, EF Dragunov) is a semi-automatic gun. It fires an old but highly effective 7.62mm x54 round and has a ten-round magazine capacity. The English translation of the entry for the Dragunov in the current Izhmash Arms catalogue states:

The 7.62mm Dragunov sniper rifle (SVD) is a sniper weapon intended to engage fleeting, moving, open and masked single targets. High workloads have had no affect on its combat features. The gas regulator increases reliability of automatics operation under hindered conditions (dirt, dust, etc). The SVD is furnished with a PSO-1M optical sight, power 3–10. The iron sight is of a sector type. The removable cheek provided on the rifle butt adds convenience when firing the rifle. The SVD is highly ergonomic and, as to convenience of holding, it stands in line with sporting rifles. The leading foreign experts recognise the SVD to be the best self-loading rifle of the twentieth century.

OK, so the English is far from perfect, but the gist is there. The Dragunov has changed little since its conception and still sells well today on the international sniper rifle market, which is testimony to its advanced design. It's also easy to use and maintain, which is in fact true of any Kalashnikov derivative; strip any such model and you'll see very few parts. It is reputed that, when Mikhail Kalashnikov first shot the UK SA80 as a guest of the British Army, he was heard to say that UK soldiers must be very smart to fire such a complicated rifle.

The most noticeable difference between the two guns mentioned here is that one is bolt-action and the other is semi-automatic. These are two very different designs in sniper weaponry. Many purists think that sniper rifles should be bolt-action, and indeed this makes the gun more stable, as nothing actually moves when the weapon is fired and there's no loss of pressure as the bolt is fixed into battery; all of the charge is retained behind the round. The cases are also ejected manually, allowing the sniper to grab them before they're thrown free to leave a telltale sign of his presence.

The semi-automatic followers, meanwhile, say that there's no perceivable loss of accuracy with their weapons, with which the sniper can follow up with a second round immediately, due to the speed of the reloading mechanism. The ejected cases can be collected, but, if one is found later, so what? If the sniper is good, he'll be long gone.

There really is no definitive answer here. The argument that the bolt-action rifle will always be more reliable, as the shooter powers the mechanism himself, is a strong one, and it's true that, in dirty conditions, a bolt-action rifle is less likely to let you down. However, when you cycle a bolt-action rifle, you have to take your eye off the target, while a semi-automatic weapon allows you to keep your eye at the scope, even if you're firing off the entire magazine.

But what would we carry? Richard Brown writes:

It was when I was being trained as a target shooter at the tender age of eighteen that I was told the aforementioned golden rule of not breaking my grip on the weapon at all costs. At the time, this rule was appropriate to a handgunner, but it's equally appropriate for a rifle shooter. My big hang-up with bolt-action guns is that you not only have to break your grip to cycle the mechanism but you actually have to remove your shooting hand all together. Couple this with the natural human reaction of lifting your head away from the scope when you cycle the mechanism and you've broken all the rules of target rifle shooting that I personally hold dear. I accept that there will be shooters of bolt-action weapons reading this who will recoil in horror at my views, believing wholeheartedly that their bolt-action gun is the most accurate in the world, and of course they're entitled to their opinion, but, as I observed when watching trained snipers firing both weapons during my recent range session with both semi-

automatic and bolt-action sniper rifles (described earlier), when shooting with semi-automatic weapons of many different types, the shooters were more at one with their guns. The symbiotic relationship between man and gun was more complete. At no point during a five-round magazine with the semi-automatic rifle did the shooters – or, indeed, I myself – once have to break our grip on the gun or take our eye from the scope. Accuracy at 600m was just over a five-inch group.

Conversely, shooting with the bolt-action gun was an awkward affair. There was much clashing of metal on metal and clicking and slithering of ammunition into the breech. The grip was broken and the eye was back and forth from the scope. The gun also produced a rattling sound – perfectly normal, as the bolt had to be manually moved, but distracting and possibly revealing. In all, there was less meshing of man and machine.

The speed of a second shot is a factor also to be considered. When considering rifles for a law-enforcement or military purpose, there's always the possibility that two shots will need to be fired in quick succession. Take, for example, the scenario of VIP protection. Here, you can never guarantee that your charge won't be attacked by two running targets, side by side, brandishing fully automatic weapons. To be able to shoot the second shot immediately after the first, one–two, is a real asset when compared to firing the first shot and then having to draw the bolt back, push it forward and reacquire the second target through the scope. There's simply no contest.

The US Army is planning to adopt a new sniper rifle in the form of the Knight's Armaments XM-110 7.62mm SASS (Semi-Automatic Sniper System). This is a similar weapon to the Knight's SR-25, newly adopted by the US Marine Corp. The rifle is a semi-automatic M4 clone which has been massively accurized and is dripping with Picatinny rails. The concept is not new and manufacturers like Bushmaster, POF USA and Heckler & Koch all make such weapons. The rationale for adopting a weapon similar to the main assault rifle is that a sniper currently stands out from his team as he obviously has a different weapon. The adoption of the XM-110 will hide his role. Additionally, the M24 is allegedly too slow for modern combat theatres. The XM-110 can be easily suppressed.

As you would expect, Remington, who currently supply the standard issue M24, are fighting back.

Non-Shooting Skills and Kit

As mentioned in the previous annexe, it was never our intention to write a technical sniper book. There are a number of very good examples of these available today that contain everything you need to know. However, while there's no point in regurgitating universally acknowledged facts for the sake of completeness, it's important to have a brief look at the non-shooting equipment and skills necessary for a sniper to operate effectively.

Even if a spotter shadows him, the sniper must be a self-sufficient fighting machine. He is often cut off from his main unit and often deployed, alone, in enemy territory. [12] This is a truly daunting experience even for the most seasoned Special Forces operative, but there is something in the sniper make up that allows him to deal with this solitude. When a soldier actually requests sniper training, therefore, it's important to test the

12. It should be noted that the contemporary peacekeeping sniper will work as part of a team (see chapter twelve).

---

applicant's psychology as well as his ability to shoot accurately over long distances.

The snipers' supplementary equipment list has changed little over the last fifty years. Although the modern-day sniper has all the benefits of modern technology, he must still possess the basic skills employed by his counterparts in wars distant in history.

Navigation and Maps

It's essential for a sniper to know where he is, and this can only be achieved by a sound understanding of map-reading and navigating skills. Since the Second World War, snipers have carried compasses and maps as standard equipment. The map enables him not only to find his current location but also to pinpoint geographical features from above, allowing him to plan ahead – for instance, in order to determine where he should be the next day, or to see potentially lethal 'dead' ground in his path, where he'll have no chance of concealing himself. He'll also add to the map as he goes, marking in good shooting spots and as he plots enemy movements, which makes him a good source of on-ground intelligence.

Today, of course, the sniper has the benefit of modern GPS (Global Positioning System) devices, but he must nevertheless be skilled in reading natural signs and a compass, as electronic equipment can never be relied upon totally.

A sound understanding of map skills also allows the sniper to create a shooting-distance card. Any good sniper can mentally create such a card, but if he has time he will draw it out. These cards usually take the form of an outer semi-circle with concentric arcs – usually at intervals of 100m to scale – moving inwards to a central point, illustrating his current position. The finished product will look a little like ripples in water.

The sniper will then estimate his distance from various key

landmarks, such as trees and rocks. A laser range-finder or even a pair of good binoculars improve accuracy here, but he should be sufficiently trained to make a fairly accurate guess.

The sniper is now well equipped and positioned to shoot quickly and very accurately. When a target walks by a particular landmark illustrated on the card, the sniper knows that the enemy soldier is – for example – exactly 750m from his shooting position, and he can quickly calibrate his sight or just make a simply elevation adjustment if, say, the gun is zeroed at 800m.

Staying Hidden

All of the navigational gear is useless, of course, if the sniper can't stay hidden from his enemy. Unlike a civilian hunter, who might wear a fluorescent jacket to avoid being shot by a fellow hunter, the sniper doesn't want anyone to see him.

Today, snipers typically wear an odd contraption called a ghillie suit. This is a full-body outfit in natural greens and browns (or even red and grey, if used in an urban environment) that will have all manner of attachments to the outer skin – for example, bits of hessian, cloth and natural material such as ferns, moss or straw, depending on where the sniper has chosen to hole up. The aim of the suit is to enable the sniper to blend with his surroundings and to break up the telltale shape of his body. A ghillie suit might be either of commercial manufacture or homemade. Even if the former, the sniper will always add his own distinctive style to the suit, depending on his current environment.

His gun, too, will be covered in netting and pieces of cloth, as it too has a shape that a sharp observer will be looking for. Netting over the front of the scope won't affect the sniper's vision, but it might prevent sunlight from glinting off the front lens.

The sniper's ghillie suit is particularly useful when he's exposed in the open. In the hands of an expert, and properly altered, the suit and its occupant are very hard to spot. Of course, as soon as such an item is conceived, there is a counter-tactic, and in this case a thermal imager will pinpoint even a well-concealed sniper via his radiating body heat. Today, however, anti-thermal suits are being developed that mask the body's thermal emissions, enabling the sniper to stay hidden even to sophisticated observation technology.

If he doesn't wish to be exposed to the elements, the sniper might also erect a temporary shelter. This will require bushcraft skills, for not only must the shelter be concealed but it must also be warm and dry. If a sniper feels the need to build such a shelter, it's invariably because he's planning to remain in the area for some time, gathering intelligence. However, it's a risky strategy to shoot from such a shelter, as it will be more difficult to conceal than his own body. Even a suppressed shot can be tracked back to an approximate location, and the enemy response – most likely involving mortar or artillery fire – will be swift and deadly.

Other natural elements can betray a sniper's location and movements. For instance, he'll need to avoid fields of animals and birds' roosting areas, as any such animal that's easily spooked could give away his position. Equally, he'll restrict his movement on ground that might leave traces of his route – i.e. soft clay, mud or snow. The latter of these can be a particular problem, especially if it freezes during the night so that, next morning, his footprints are exposed for all to see.

Other Equipment

The sniper must be able to defend himself if the battle moves a little too close for him to be able to use his rifle. If a patrol squad is almost on top of him, his rifle will be too unwieldy for effective combat. To this end, since the Second World War, snipers have always carried supplementary defence equipment. A modern sniper will always carry a sub-machine gun, ideally a model that can collapse down for easy transport. In the 1940s, the British sniper would typically have carried a 9mm Sten gun, which was the only suitable weapon of the time. Today the choice is wider, but the criteria are the same: the gun will need to be small and light, be quick to load and have a high rate of fire. Bearing this in mind, possible options might be the Heckler & Koch MK5K PDW or perhaps an older gun such as the Ingram MAC 10, which could also be effectively suppressed. These guns aren't much bigger than handguns but offer firepower of considerably greater flexibility.

The sniper will also carry a pistol as a last-defence weapon. This will usually take the form of the standard-issue military handgun of his country of origin, but there is an argument for carrying one of the newer 'wonder-nines' that carry upwards of seventeen 9mm rounds in a single magazine. Revolvers were certainly carried many years ago, but it's rare to see them today in a military environment. (This is actually a shame, as a good, long-barrelled Magnum used in parallel with a sub-compact 9mm SMG is a good combination. The only possible issue is the need to carry ammunition of two different calibres.)

Snipers also often carry one or more grenades, either of a high-explosive or anti-personnel type. One of these thrown into an approaching squad of men is a sure-fire way to generate chaos.

ANNEXE C

Innovations in
Sniper Rifles

We've mentioned – and, in some cases, discussed in detail – various sniper rifles over the course of this book. Indeed, it's difficult to write a book like this without such references. One corollary of sniper-rifle development that's worthy of analysis is the amazing firearms innovations that this has brought. We're not talking here about the difference between a smooth-bored musket and a rifled weapon but about more radical changes and inventions, some of which are now standard in sniper weapons and have since cropped up on infantry guns and some which, while appearing groundbreaking at the time, have disappeared.

The dawn of true, purist sniping (i.e. using a rifle and scope to increase the aiming range of a gun beyond the capability of the naked eye) can arguably be tied down to the invention of one particular gun, a radical machine that should have taken a war by storm but instead died as technology took a swerve and moved on.

The gun in question is the Whitworth sniper rifle from the American Civil War.

The Whitworth rifle came along during a period that many shooting enthusiasts think of as the golden era of firearms. New inventions and concepts were common and the science of ballistics was a hot topic. In 1854, an engineer named Joseph Whitworth who had made significant improvements on the design of the screw thread was commissioned by the British government to examine the possibility of creating a weapon that could compete against the standard British Army .577 Enfield. Such a weapon had to be capable of being mass-produced and still meet contemporary military standards of maintenance and durability.

Whitworth was partnered with army staff and a technician named Westley Richards, who had already come up with a radical idea for increasing the range of a gun, based on a new take on rifling. He envisaged an octagonal barrel, with a bullet to match. In order to impart spin, the straight barrel would be twisted, effectively turning the whole barrel into one big 'rifle'.

Whitworth made Richards's dream a reality and produced a rifle with a hexagonal twisted barrel and a bullet to match. The bullet was easy to load, as the gun was a muzzle-loading weapon; once the shape of the bullet had been lined up with that of the muzzle – like a hexagonal hole-and-peg toy – the ramrod could be used to push the round home as normal. Whitworth reduced the calibre to .451 inches, which he deemed to be the optimum size for maximum muzzle velocity.

When fitted with a scope, the rifle was accurate to an astonishing 1,500 yards. Of course, in the 1860s, scopes were nothing like the ones of today. In the early days of shooting, they were made of brass and stretched almost the entire length of the gun, resembling full-size telescopes.

The British government wasn't convinced that the Whitworth

rifle was indeed the successor to the old Lee-Enfield model, but they did concede that the weapon shot extremely well. It was, however, prone to fouling, but this was considered a tolerable weakness. The main stumbling block in the path of its development was that the government didn't consider the weapon sufficiently robust for military use. Nevertheless, as the rifle was so superbly accurate, the military (unusually) decided that there might well be some use for it, and Whitworth eventually delivered 8,000 units.

Interestingly, the weapon did achieve some level of fame when Queen Victoria opened a new gun range with a single, highly accurate shot from a Whitworth. This was an interesting use of the weapon, a little like Queen Elizabeth II today opening a defence exhibition in London by firing a precision guided missile out over the capital.

The decision to let Queen Victoria open the show with a Whitworth unequivocally placed the rifle on a pedestal, representing the very height of cutting-edge weapons technology of the day. It would certainly have been noted in the British and foreign press which rifle the Queen had used, and an artist's impression, or even an early photograph, might have accompanied the article – a fine marketing coup for Whitworth. Of course, the Queen didn't actually lay her hands on the gun, no doubt for fear of damaging her fine clothing with powder burns or oil; instead, the weapon was firmly clamped and lined up perfectly with the target and Her Royal Highness pulled a delicate string of silk that had been tied to the trigger. It must have been quite a spectacle, but equally it represented a golden age of shooting in Britain.

Despite its high-profile start in life, the Whitworth rifle was never fully accepted into British service, due to a combination of the traditional British fear of a new infantry gun and rumours of its propensity for fouling. In the 1860s, however, Whitworths began to appear in the hands of the Confederate Army during the American Civil War. Such a transatlantic jump wasn't uncommon, as many weapons were supplied for the war through British gun dealers. Colt even established a manufacturing facility in London, and today collectors actively seek Colt pistols bearing London markings. Ships laden with guns arrived regularly in America to resupply the Union Forces, and rebel ships slipped around blockades to supply Confederate troops. Indeed, many of the landed gentry in England greatly sympathised with the wealthier families in the southern states. The English country gentleman felt a very real kinship with the very prosperous colonials on the other side of the Atlantic, for two reasons: first, the British elite couldn't resist an armed skirmish, from the perspective of the underdog, and second, they felt passionately that the privileged lifestyle of large country manors and servants (i.e. slaves) should be preserved. Many of the top few in England therefore thought it quite the done thing to do all they could to supply their kindred spirits with small arms with which to ward off the Union troops. This ridiculous state of affairs simply served to extend an already bloody war waged thousands of miles away.

The Confederate Army, through its agents in England, arranged the purchase of over 13,000 Whitworths from the factory in Manchester. (Restrictive export control laws were 140 years away!) Of these rifles, 5,400 were destined for southern troops, and we can assume that the remainder were to stay in the hands of loyal civilians, although we suspect that the number of rifles that actually made it through is actually very small. Nevertheless, the Whitworth was probably the world's first purpose-built gun, its design driven by a desire for accuracy above all other criteria. (This overriding search for perfect accuracy is also true of the designs of today's sniper rifles, which don't have the robust qualities of their infantry cousins.) For this reason, the Whitworth has certainly earned an entry in these pages.

Another issue – and one that has always been a scourge of the Special Forces shooter – is that you can never have a silent gun. By 'silent', we don't mean the report of a firing gun but the mechanism of the weapon itself. If you fire a suppressed semi- or fully automatic weapon, it's impossible to hide the noise of the gun cycling. Admittedly, the gun *is* very quiet, but the sound of the bolt ratcheting back and forth at high speed is always audible. This, of course, poses a very real problem for the sniper who needs to chamber his weapon in absolute silence. Military ears are trained to hear the sound of weapons cocking, and in a jungle environment, for example, the metallic click of a large-calibre rifle being cocked is unmistakable. Now, it's true that the target will probably be too far away to hear this, but the sniper can't take that chance.

To this end, some manufacturers – particularly Heckler & Koch – produce sniper rifles fitted with silent bolt-closing devices. The mechanism is based on the old bolt-closing (or bolt-forcing!) device first conceived by Colt for the M16, which was possibly one of the most questionable gadgets ever invented for a gun. The principle was that the bolt had grooves cut in it that matched the teeth of a plunger in the side of the gun. Should the bolt then be jammed open – by dirt, for instance – in the heat of battle, the soldier would repeatedly push this plunger inwards, which would propel the bolt forward as the teeth caught in its grooves. After several plunges, the bolt and a new round would be back in battery. Needless to say, this mechanism was only to be used in a truly life-threatening situation.

Manufacturers of sniper weapons later realised that a finely tuned version of the groove/plunger system could be used as a slow, but silent, method of pushing a bolt into battery and load a round. From a terrible invention came a brilliant solution to a different problem.

Another great invention, standard on most (but not all) sniper rifles, is the free-floating barrel. This was developed in response to the need for accuracy even in adverse environmental conditions, which take their toll on weapons – not just on the metalwork (which must be protected from rust) but on the stock, too. When weapons of war were made predominantly of wood, this was of course a much greater issue, as in damp and warm conditions wood will expand and contract. If the barrel of a gun is in direct contact with the wooden stock, the movement of the wood can push extremely hard on the barrel and throw it off true. If you were firing a Lee-Enfield at 100m, this probably wouldn't make much difference, but if you were firing a sniper rifle at 1,000m, a small deviation at the business end of the gun might mean you'd miss the shot. This was the problem behind the invention of free-floating barrels, which are fixed very solidly into the receiver and stand proud of any of the exterior bodywork of the gun. This means that if the wood or, even, polymer moves due to environmental conditions, the barrel stays straight. It's a simple but effective solution.

Another invention that sprang from the need to shoot a man at great distance is the *mil-dot*, which is the mark that appears on the reticle (i.e. crosshairs) of the sniper scope that enables the shooter to gauge the distance to an object of estimated height or width, taking some of the guesswork out of aiming. Obviously, if your sight is zeroed at 100m, you won't be able to aim straight at a target that you estimate to be at least 300m away, as a straight shot at this distance will put the round at the target's feet. Instead, you must elevate the barrel to counter for the effect of gravity and the slowing velocity of the bullet. Designed around the measurement unit the milliradian – a sub-unit of the radian, the SI unit of angle – the mil-dot reticle was once an exclusive accessory to the most expensive sniper rifles but has now become a standard feature of very modern assault rifles. Take, for example, the integral scope of a modern assault rifle, displayed below. This sight is zeroed at 200m:

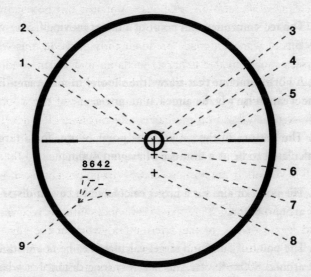

At first sight, this might appear to be a thoroughly confusing object to look through (although, of course, a real scope wouldn't have all of these lines and numbers!), but this illustration demonstrates a clear example of pure sniper technology making its way down to the battlefield infantryman.

1. The recommended point of aim at a moving target traversing left to right at an approximate speed of 7.5kph. A shot lined up with this side of the small ring should allow the shooter to make a direct hit on the target, effectively anticipating the position of the moving target when the bullet reaches the point of impact.

2. The aiming point for a stationary target at 200m. At distances of under 200m, the weapon's iron sights can be used.

3. The ring represents the size of a man – assumed to be 1.75m tall – standing at a distance of 400m.

4. The recommended aim point of a target moving from right to left.

5. A horizontal line that allows the shooter to make sure that the weapon isn't being aimed at an angle.

6. The bottom of the circle is the point of aim for a target calculated to be at a distance of around 400m.

7. The point of aim for a target calculated to be at a distance of around 600m.

8. The point of aim for a target calculated to be at a distance of around 800m. Note: This is a very long distance at which to engage targets with an assault rifle, but the fact that such a mark is present is testimony to the increased capabilities that a basic scope gives the shooter. There's no question that rifle ammunition at 800m will be lethal, but it's extremely difficult for the human eye to aim a gun at such a distant target.

9. These small lines represent the size of a man at 800, 600, 400 and 200m, respectively. The shooter measures the size of the target from the small line to the large line under the numbers 8 6 4 2.

The purpose of this annexe is essentially to demonstrate how influential sniper rifles, and their creation, have been on the world of firearms. The precision performance of a purpose-built sniper rifle will never fully be replicated in a standard combat weapon, but man's desire to make a super-accurate gun, from the Whitworth to free-floating-barrel rifles, has ultimately led to a simpler version of the technology filtering its way down to the basic rifle. We're coming close to the point where we can genuinely ask, 'Where is there left for guns to go?'

Without doubt, ammunition is getting smaller. The days of soldiers shooting .75-calibre balls at one another are long gone, and it's only a matter of time before old die-hards such as the 9mm x19 and the 7.62mm x51 are consigned to the pages of history.

What we can say with some certainty is that the developments of the next generation of sniper rifle for the twenty-first century will one day make their way down to basic guns. The question is, will assault rifles one day become so accurate and technically brilliant that the sniper rifle will become extinct?

The Killer in Shadows – The Art of a Sniper

This short annexe exists to provide an insight into the mindset of both sniper and victim, to explain a moment of anxiety that exists for each.

The Washington Sniper incident involved a 'sniper' rather than a professional sniper. The killings were perpetrated by a man who worked the fear conjured by the sniper but wasn't a professionally trained sniper shooting from a considerable distance. However, as a concealed marksman – the killer in shadows – John Allen Muhammad was able to disrupt a large urban area such as Washington and inject chaos into the normal working pattern of people's lives, in effect creating a 'sniper effect' rather than engaging in 'sniper activity'.

But how did the Washington sniper *feel*? Charles Moose explained that he was disappointed by the justification given by the killer – and that, really, is what he was: a killer, not a sniper; a man who used the 'sniper effect', but not the skills of a sniper, to ensure that his job was carried out successfully and to escape afterwards into the shadows. In fact, our interview with Charles Moose has led us to believe that the Washington sniper *wanted* to be captured, hence the notes he left for the police; a sniper wouldn't leave clues. He wouldn't – like Scorpio in *Dirty Harry* did – leave notes and bargain with the authorities. So the Washington sniper is an amateur, like Scorpio; a man with little justification beyond the ranting rationalisations of a madman.

But, you might ask, *what about the professional sniper? How does he feel?*

It's not in his remit to feel.

OK. But does he have feelings?

Yes, and sometimes they are investigated and explored, but only much later. He is, after all, a highly trained professional.

What about highly trained professionals who have to keep terrible secrets?

Such as what?

Such as killing somebody like a president, not taking the credit and bottling up inside the magnitude of the job? Surely it must eat them up, even kill them eventually?

In point of fact, there was a French sailor who claimed some time after the Battle of Trafalgar that he was indeed the man who shot Lord Nelson. This has been documented by other sniper enthusiasts as proof that the man survived Trafalgar and that it was the Royal Navy's pride that led it to propound the story that Lord Nelson's murder was avenged. However, this theory is hopelessly flawed. The sniper(s) who shot at Lord Nelson were shooting from a dead ship and wound up the same way themselves. And, besides, the bragging of killing Lord Nelson is in contradiction to the anatomy of a sniper.

But how does it feel? This is one aspect of a sniper that no one but the shooter can ever really know; it's too big a question. But somewhere out there, somebody *does* know how that feels and how – if possible – to deal with those feelings.

ANNEXE E

The Mentality of a Sniper

As our interview with a sniper revealed, earlier in this book, a sniper – professional or otherwise – doesn't always have the opportunity to prepare for the job in hand. The rooftop nutter will most likely pick a victim just because of what they look like (and, of course, his own prejudice), while the military sniper cannot pre-empt the situation in which he'll find himself.

Taking the military sniper as our example for this annexe, let's assume that he's trained well enough to think on his feet, to adapt to extreme – and highly dangerous – situations. If he believes that a scenario is simple or similar to one he's experienced before, he'll make errors because every situation – especially in-theatre – is different. Every situation is new, with its own exclusive problems and intricacies. These could be based around the difficulty of the shot or job – for instance, locating the perfect location to lie low. Location can be as much an enemy to the sniper as the enemy himself. What about the blast of the desert sand across the scope and the lack of cover in a desert scenario? Or the snakes and spiders of the jungle?

A military sniper is highly trained, not just in his skill with a rifle but in military techniques as well. Only when the fundamental survival skills have been learned can the techniques be finely tuned and the trained sniper be deployed.

But it's not whether or not a sniper has been trained; it's whether or not he's able to wade through swamps of chest-high mud and then pull himself up a two-foot climbing frame, crying bitterly because he can't escape the mud, and, when he does, he slips on the frame, back into the ooze. But the commanding officer is screaming for results, so he tries and tries again, because this is military fitness; this is survival training.

Then, of course, there's hostage training. Can he survive being kept in a room for days, deprived of food, believing that the enemy has captured him, not his own people? Will he crack? Will he give away the secrets he's been sworn to keep? When he's hundreds of feet above the sea, blindfolded and tied up in a bag, will he break? 'Tell us the truth or we'll drop you into the sea. Fish food, my friend!' So he doesn't talk and is thrown off the helicopter, landing on the ground a foot below. The penny drops. The test is over. Get over it.

This is one aspect of training within the Special Forces. It is not based on true stories but is included to illustrate the point that the sniper must be a special quality of soldier before he can be made a sniper. He must then be highly trained and have reached a high level of professionalism before he can be applied to the task of sniping.

So now let's look a little more closely at the mentality of a sniper, because, in order to perform the tasks he does, he must be focused, completely in tune with his environment – to the extent of being part of it – and totally dedicated to the main objective of the operation: eliminating target.

The sniper isn't jumpy; his breathing is regulated, his senses alert, but, at the same time, he is relaxed. He is physically fit, yes, but more importantly he is mentally fit, perhaps more secure in his mind than the average soldier. But why be a sniper? Well, you might ask, why be a soldier in the first place?

It's in the blood. The desire to become an expert in a chosen field, within a profession, is an elemental part of the sniper's make-up, as our sniper explained earlier. He doesn't see people (well, not right away, at least); he sees targets. Sniping is a cold, detached job. OK, you could be looking at somebody for days through a scope, learning their daily pattern, seeing the whites of their eyes, but the target is the job, and it's up to the sniper to take him out and then get out. It's as simple as that.

The concept of the 'target' is an interesting one. In the earlier interview, our sniper admits that he sees a target but that it's only later that he thinks of him as a human being. Does this mean that, once the job is over, once the target has been taken out, the sniper will wake up in a cold sweat in the middle of the night, knowing that he's taken somebody else's life?

It is not as clear cut as this, and every sniper deals with his own demons in his own way. The most important thing to appreciate is that the military sniper is there for the good of the free world. He carries his own mental baggage as happily as his dedication to his unit and his family waiting for him at home.

Some people crave a difficult and demanding lifestyle; it's what they thrive on; and the men and women of the Special Forces – and the regular British Army, too – are trained in a vast number of skills in order to be effective in many different scenarios within their day-to-day work.

It's important to look at the wider picture when discussing military snipers of any nation, for there is much more to their job than they are given credit for.

ANNEXE F

Counter-sniper Tactics

> 'Bond felt the whisky beginning to melt the coiled
> nerves in his stomach. "Now then, Liselotte, how in hell
> are you going to get out of this fix?"'
>
> IAN FLEMING, *THE LIVING DAYLIGHTS*

Throughout this book, we have analysed in some considerable detail the damage a well-trained sniper can inflict on his chosen enemy, and you might be forgiven for thinking that there is no defence against this perfect symbiotic blend of man and destructive machine. If a sniper has his quarry in his sights, this is probably the truth, but the target can minimise his personal risk and fight back once the sniper has made his presence known.

Anti-sniper warfare is a tricky business, but in this respect the sniper is like any other good weapon; the only certainty in the battlefield is that someone will someday conceive a way to beat that weapon. Countermeasures against all forms of weapons are becoming ever more sophisticated, but technical superiority alone won't guarantee a defence against the sniper. The best method is to fool or outsmart him.

But let's look at technology first. What kind of anti-sniper gear is available? Can the sniper be defeated by the microchip? In short, yes, he can, but not until he's fired at least one round. The obvious problem with this is that the high-value target is possibly dead, and whether or not the sniper is later discovered frankly makes little difference, other than meaning that he can then be executed or prosecuted.

If a sniper attack is probable, one basic solution is to invest in a sniper-detection system. Such systems (described below) are expensive but do give a good chance of finding and eliminating the sniper, even if he's fired his first shot. Finding a sniper is all about acceptable losses (and whether or not the President of the free world is an acceptable loss is a debate for another book), but the fact remains that often a sniper cannot be caught until he's fired his first shot.

Sniper-detection systems take the form of acoustic-location devices. Such technology has been used by armed forces to find artillery for many years. Indeed, in the recent Gulf War Operation Telic, such a system was used to great effect to defeat Iraqi main battle tanks. The military commanders determined that the enemy tanks had to fire shells to find the correct range to Coalition tanks, and the firing of these ranging shots was detected by UK military acoustic systems, the location triangulated and the resulting co-ordinates sent at lightning speed to UK targeting computers. The Coalition artillerymen therefore knew exactly where to place their shells in order to achieve a one-shot/one-kill ratio. Such a system is ingenious and makes it unnecessary to expend a lot of ammunition, but it's a gamble, as the other side must fire first, before any action can be taken. However, when the Iraqis' elderly

Cold War-surplus Russian T-55 tanks were pitched against Challengers 2s and AS90 self-propelled guns, the odds lay very much in the Coalition favour.

Sniper-detection systems work a little like the above artillery example, but with subtle differences. The detection system itself will comprise a central processor, which is remotely linked to several detectors, or microphones. Each detector will be programmed to cover a certain area, and their detection ranges will overlap, in much the same way that ripples merge in water, in order to cover a wide area with no gaps.

If a shot is fired, the sniper-detection system detects the initial 'crack-thump' of the gun and the sonic shock wave of the bullet passing through the air. By knowing both the location of the firing weapon and the trajectory of the round, pinpointing exactly where the sniper shot originated is relatively simple. If such a system is used in a theatre of war, the general area can then be bombarded with mortars or an aerial attack. If the situation is one of defence in an urban, highly populated, civilian area, deploying the closest counter-terrorist unit to the location of the rifle shot will maximise the chances of catching the killer.

Technology in counter-sniper operations is moving at a considerable speed and the latest versions of sniper-detection systems can even be vehicle- or man-mounted. The advantage this gives is that, if a sniper takes a shot at a moving motorcade, even as the VIP cars are speeding away, the exact location of the shooter can be calculated simultaneously by numerous such devices. Even a suppressed weapon won't help the sniper significantly, as the system will have tracked the path of the bullet and made a guess at its origination, possibly even narrowing it down to a single building.

Although sniper-detection systems and their skilled use are becoming increasingly common, they're expensive and not always practical. Other, more basic skills are needed in order to challenge an enemy sniper.

The potential targets must do everything they can to make the sniper's job harder. It's better, after all, to try to fox him before he takes a shot than to catch him after he has killed. This can be achieved by deploying concealment and decoys, making it hard for the sniper to find and hit a high-value target, to make him waste time and, hopefully, reveal his location.

The first and most obvious step is one that Lord Nelson should have taken. Without doubt, Nelson was targeted as a result of his flamboyant uniform, and this is equally true of Timothy Murphy's targets at the Battle of Saratoga. It was only by the turn of the twentieth century that military forces finally realised that an officer emblazoned with gold braid was a prime target for ever more accurate small arms. Slowly, uniforms became more generic, and by D-Day in 1944 the only identifying rank marks on some soldiers' uniforms were small white symbols on their helmets, effectively disguising the high-value targets – the officers – among the lower ranks. Of course, in such a scenario the sniper still has his pick of machine gunners and radio operators, but those in command are far less obvious.

Equally, increasingly covert methods of communication have made the sniper's job harder. Encrypted communications and other stealthy methods of passing on commands make the sniper's ability to gain valuable intelligence limited.

Another consideration is how the sniper receives his instructions. While satellite technology and high-level imaging equipment are used with increasing frequency on the battlefield, these super-smart devices can be deceived relatively simply. As a jet plane passes overhead, for instance, the pilot and, possibly, his camera have fleeting seconds in which to identify an image correctly. More often than not, this is achieved by analysing the object's shadow, which gives a clearer identity of a ground-based asset than an overhead picture would.

Once the enemy gun or vehicle has been identified, a reaction force can be deployed, and this might comprise air attack, ground forces or snipers. You can imagine the surprise of the sniper when he cautiously advances on the battery of field howitzers or attack helicopters under netting to find that his colleagues in the air have been duped by a collection of junk that has been cleverly arranged to cast the shadow of a howitzer on the ground. Having been sucked into the trap, his shock is compounded when he realises that he's activated ground sensors laid to catch him.

What follows is a tale describing possibly the best example of visual deception we have ever seen and demonstrates effectively how laterally the deception artists in the armed forces can think. This story actually has nothing to do with snipers, and doesn't even contain a reference to a rifle, but we hope the reader will indulge us.

The Canadian Air Force fly F16 fast jets. In a stroke of genius, they have begun to paint highly realistic three-dimensional cockpits on the bottom of the fuselage, directly under the real cockpit. The theory is that, despite the vast array of technical detection equipment fitted to a modern fighter, the pilot still uses his eyes. At truly outrageous passing speeds of Mach 2, both pilots have only fleeting glimpses of each other's aircraft. The enemy pilot's eyes will register the rough shape of the F16 fighter, which way it was facing and heading. Given the direction of the pass, the enemy pilot will know that the laws of nature dictate that the Canadian plane is likely to pull away in a certain direction, so when the fighter pulls away in exactly the opposite direction, and in a manner that should tear the aircraft apart, the enemy fighter pilot is left very confused.

When the enemy pilot takes his mental snapshot in that high-speed F16, his brain subconsciously registers the exact position of the fighter. Of course, what he actually saw was a plane with a fake cockpit painted on to the fuselage, which is how the F16 can pull off in exactly the opposite direction to the one he was expecting. Realising his mistake, he hurriedly resets his brain and begins to reacquire the turning F16 – but it's too late; the ten seconds of total confusion the fake cockpit created has given the F16 time to lock and fire a missile.

Now that we've successfully fooled the sniper, how do we catch him? Even if he's fired his shot and we had no advance warning that he was coming, we now know roughly where he is and must act quickly or he will disappear, maybe to come back and haunt us at a later date.

If we have some idea of where the shot came from, we can send two squads out on either side of the estimated shooting path. These hunter-killer troops can then slowly come together in an arc and form a wall behind the sniper. As they then push back to their base, the sniper should theoretically be trapped and flushed out.

This tactic has a good chance of success, as the sniper will be indoctrinated to fire and move very slowly away, so as not to accidentally betray his position. He won't just shoot, stand up and run away. However, only a fast-moving sniper will be able to escape the two closing approaches of the enemy.

To block off the sniper's escape route is to deny him one of his basic requirements for a successful operation. If he feels that troop defensive positions are arranged in such a way that he'll be trapped on firing, he might even decide to abort the operation and slip away.

The modern sniper must also be aware of ground-based radar. Several such units will be established around a large camp, their beams interlocking in exactly the same way as the detection fields of the acoustic detectors. Capable of picking out an animal the size of a fox at 1,000m, such radar equipment makes the sniper's job very difficult, and again his command structure might order him to abort if the defences at the enemy base are too strong.

Another method of defence is to bring in a second sniper. This tactic is explored graphically in chapter six, but it's just as relevant on the modern battlefield. Defensive resources here are always limited, and having an expert on hand to say 'I'd shoot from there or there' can be invaluable.

If a sniper who has successfully targeted your base several times is plaguing you, a counter-sniper is probably one of your best options. The main benefit with this defensive measure is that the enemy sniper should be unaware that he is being stalked. Like the attacking sniper, the counter-sniper also has a very fixed job, but he doesn't have to select high-value targets, he doesn't have to be concerned about the noise of his sniper shot and, if he can't make the shot, he can call in support from the base. If the enemy sniper suspects another shooter is stalking him, he will almost certainly retreat, as his original mission will be almost impossible to achieve if he has to spend every moment watching his back.

Chapter one briefly explored alternative targets for the modern sniper. These can all be protected with relative ease if the threat of a sniper is real. Banks can be constructed behind which to conceal helicopters and vehicles. Natural terrain can be utilised to deny the enemy sniper an easy shot by blocking his field of vision. However, there is no guaranteed protection against a determined sniper; all you can do is make sure that you give him the hardest shot possible. Keep targets in your camp visually obscured and level the earth for a square mile outside your perimeter. Leave the sniper nowhere to go. Make sure that your high-value targets are well protected. If you have time, plant ground-based sensors and deploy ground-based radars and thermal imagers. If you're in an urban environment, make sure that high buildings are off limits so that any unauthorised figure will stand out. Also, have an acoustic-detection system up and running so that, if he strikes, you can move fast.

Finally, it always pays to have a good sniper on standby. A single bullet is by far the most cost-effective and efficient way to remove an enemy shooter. If your marksman is good, he might even be able to predict the enemy's intentions and solve your problem before you take a single round of incoming fire.

James Bond said wearily, 'OK. With any luck it'll cost me my double-O number. But tell the Head of Station not to worry. That girl won't do any more sniping. Probably lost her left hand. Certainly broke her nerve for that kind of work...'

IAN FLEMING, *THE LIVING DAYLIGHTS*

Author Interview – David L Robbins

David L Robbins's name might not be instantly recognisable to British readers, yet many of his books, such as *The End of War* and *Scorched Earth*, have graced the UK bestseller lists. His novel *Last Citadel* (Orion, 2003) is a superb work of fiction based around the Battle of Kursk and includes a bibliography of over thirty published histories Robbins used in his research for the novel.

With this in mind, it's not surprising to find that Robbins was once a journalist. He is now a teacher of creative writing at Virginia Commonwealth University, and his six novels have earned him the mantle of one of the best contemporary novelists working in America today. As mentioned elsewhere, his 1999 international bestseller *War of the Rats* was turned into the popular movie *Enemy at the Gates*, starring Jude Law and Ed Harris.

In order that the interpretation of the sniper in fiction – both in novel and on film – could be covered, we include here an interview with David L Robbins concerning his novel *War of the Rats*, which explores the background research that he conducted for the project and how it was treated as a blockbuster movie.

Four of your six novels concern the Second World War. Why the fascination?

I don't particularly have a fascination with the Second World War. My preoccupation is with grand settings for my characters. If you want to know what a character is going to do and what he's made of, have him fall in love, or have him troubled and tested. Perhaps shoot at him, test him, boil him in a cauldron. Great historical cauldrons are what I look for. The Second World War is one setting that fits the bill. Plus, I look for backdrops that allow my readers to learn something; the Eastern Front of the Second World War has been badly overlooked in the West in both fiction and history, so I set four books there, starting with the battles of Stalingrad.

What did you think of the movie *Enemy at the Gates*? Although a big movie, it was nowhere near as detailed or exciting as your novel *War of the Rats*.

It was poor, frankly. The research in the movie was abysmal; the verisimilitude was way off. The writers and producers took a perfectly tragic and compelling true story of a sniper duel and a real love story and junked them up with inanities and laughably bad history, ignoring fact. I think the movie did a disservice to the courage of the real fighters Zaitsev and Chernova, and to the battle of Stalingrad as a whole. I hope it doesn't do so much damage that the movie industry refuses to revisit the Eastern Front. Many immense and pivotal battles were fought there and there are great stories about it to be told.

Where do you see your work going?

I see my work staying in the realms of history and conflict, but I also want to branch out to more literary pieces like *Scorched Earth*. However, I'll flip though history and choose another interesting epoch to explore for a while.

Your work seems radically different to a lot of other American writers. How do you explain this?

I think I'm one of only a handful of American writers who believes you can tell a rousing, good, exciting tale with beautiful language and insight. Too often, American publishers and writers fall for the easy bits of raw action and dialogue to tell their tales. I respect my stories too much to lay them out in anything but their finest forms. I love words, and I love the riddles and vagaries of the heart. Moral quandaries, terror, courage, memory, loyalty, adoration, loss – how can any machine, mystery or autopsy be better than an exploration of these? I trust words and insight to be the masters of my stories, and I allow action and dialogue to serve them.

What, or who, influences your writing?

My influences are few, really. I start with the daily news. Next comes history. Finally, the writers whose work I try to emulate – and by that I mean the effort of their work, their adherence to voice and pace, not their style; I've laboured hard to establish my own style. Include Steinbeck for his courage, Hemingway for his concision, Faulkner for his experimentation with form, Tolstoy and Nabokov for their breadth and George MacDonald Fraser for his wit and accuracy.

As somebody who teaches creative writing, what's the most important thing to take into account when writing a novel?

I teach novel writing, and I tell my students never to write unless they're at their best. Don't commit to the page anything but your utmost. Writing isn't a sport or a relationship where you can do it again or say you're sorry. Writing, especially the long form of a novel, means you're putting down words and ideas that are indelible. They will be read and you won't be there to explain them or excuse them. You must, every minute and every word, be on top of your game because of the permanence of the page.

How can you teach somebody to write a novel? Surely, somebody either has or doesn't have the imagination?

Everyone has imagination, and most writers have a decent story. These aren't why a writer will fail. A particular writer won't ever write a good book because he lacks other things, such as time, discipline, craft, passion, money to pay for food while he writes. You'd be amazed at the mundane reasons that stand in the way of writing. I teach my students two things: write boldly and write often.

Have you thought about writing non-fiction? You seem to enjoy researching themes quite thoroughly.

Not really. I do enjoy the research and the travel to do it, but my real passion is storytelling. I like making things up, walking make-believe people through authentic worlds. The research helps me build those worlds, but the folks who people those worlds and times come out of my heart, head and experience. That's what jazzes me the most: creating, more than finding out.

Going back to *War of the Rats*, how did you start your research?

The first thing I did was go to the Library of Congress in Washington, DC. This was in 1988, before the internet and the ability to type in a name and download a virtual library of information on any topic. I found mention of Zaitsev's memoirs, then located the book in the stacks. It was in Russian, of course, so I made a copy of the entire manuscript. Then I returned to the University of Richmond, one of my hometown colleges, and hired a Russian professor – a wonderful man from Moscow named Fedya who became the model for the young poet of the same name in *War of the Rats* – to read it in English into a cassette recorder. From there, I devoured everything I could get my hands on regarding Stalingrad.

You obviously write from the point of view that Zaitsev was a real person. Do you honestly believe that, or is it a romantic notion you wish to believe?

Of course he was real. I spoke to him several times. I travelled to Kiev in 1990 and interviewed him, then had three more chats with him on the phone long-distance from the States, with Fedya on the line translating. What an odd notion that Zaitsev might not have existed! I wasn't aware such a line of thought had developed. He passed away in 1993, I believe. He was very famous in the Soviet Union; they named high schools after him.

Why did you decide to write about snipers?

I didn't. I decided to write a fantastic love story set in the rubble and horror of Stalingrad, based on a true and harrowing tale. It so happens that both of the lovers, Zaitsev and Tania, were snipers, as was the antagonist Thorwald, sent to kill Zaitsev. But *War of the Rats* is about so much more than sniping. Had they been sappers, the book would have been about bomb removal and tunnel digging.

What research did you do into sniping?

I found a retired Navy Seabee at a local gun shop who collected rifles of the Second World War. He owned the two rifles featured in the novel, the Mauser and the Mosin Nagant. He taught me everything about them: how to take them apart and how to shoot them. I had never in my life held a rifle, much less fired one. We went to a target range for an entire day and he handed me the two guns and gave me plenty of instruction. I also read everything I could find on the topic. I also was fortunate to interview a few ex-snipers from the Vietnam era who gave me the best and most chilling insights. Then, when I spoke with Vasha, I was prepared to ask insightful and direct questions, which he appreciated.

Has *War of the Rats* changed your opinion of snipers? If so, how?

If you study enough about war, you draw few moral distinctions about how men choose to kill one another. Snipers are terribly effective not only at killing but at sapping an enemy's morale and confidence that there exists anywhere safe on a battlefield. The value of this is so great, from a military standpoint, that the grimness of the kill can easily be excused and the sniper granted amnesty from judgement. His measure of courage is ample, surely, but courage and sacrifice are not rare in battle.

Do you feel we need snipers in the present day? The Iraq War, for example?

Yes, of course, but not in Iraq. There, the mission was not to kill but to subdue. Killing is only one tool and should always be the last resort. The insurgents remaining in Iraq must be convinced to put down their guns and turn their energies to the peaceful administration of their land. Force is the best way to convince them to stop fighting and killing. Still, we weren't in Iraq to halt a threat to the world as we were in the Second World War; we were there to liberate the same people we were combating. Every dead Iraqi was one more family filled with hatred for the West. We struggled in Iraq for hearts as well as bodies, and we could have done if our focus there had been only on stopping those hearts.

The sniper is too effective a killer. He has no direct engagement with his target. An enemy can't lay down his weapon before a sniper. This option had to stay open in Iraq in order to keep enemy casualties to the absolute minimum needed to accomplish the military goals there.

What is your opinion of the sniper at the movies – for example Scorpio in *Dirty Harry*?

Sniping in movies has always been reduced to a simplistic formula: shoot someone from a hiding spot, over a long distance, using a crosshair. Nothing about Hollywood's efforts has ever come close to capturing the dedication, nerve and raw marksmanship of the best military snipers – not even the movie *Sniper*. Too often, sniping in the movies is the earmark of a madman or a coward. Not many of them live long.

How did you get into the mentality of a sniper for *War of the Rats*?

Interviews. Reading. Shooting. Travelling. And, most importantly, empathy and imagination – the skills of a writer.

Are you a shooter yourself? Indeed, have you ever shot a rifle?

I'm not a long-distance marksman, though I enjoy sporting clays. I have a Beretta single-barrel twelve-gauge.

Will you write about snipers again?

No.

It is interesting that Robbins wishes to write only fiction, as he bases so much of his writing on meticulous research. His stance on the movie interpretation of his novel *War of the Rats* is understandable, but life goes on. It's interesting to note, though, that Hollywood will always twist well-researched facts to suit its own ideology rather than change its own ideology to suit the well-researched facts. In the face of this approach to film-making, the sniper will always be misrepresented on screen and quality writers such as David L Robbins will move on to other subjects.

Choose Your Weapon

Hopefully, while reading this book, if one thing has become clear it's that the world of the sniper and his rifle is truly global. There are so many sniper rifles on the market today that it's almost impossible to keep count and to keep pace with new technology. With so many standard military assault rifles being 'sniperised', it's just too difficult to determine how many sniper rifles are currently available to military and law-enforcement organisations or the civilian buyer. So how do you choose which gun is best for you? Well, for a civilian shooter, it's easy. You pick the one you like best.

If you're a government buyer, however, the acquiring of weaponry is a more complex issue. Like most purchasers, you'll probably look at what's being produced by your own country. So many nations now make some form of rifle that's capable of shooting over long ranges, but equally there are many that have absolutely no indigenous manufacturing process and buy everything in. This is not an unenviable position for a country to be in, however, as it doesn't require the expense of running a factory, but equally there is no export base. Such countries aren't necessarily small and poor, either; their position with regard to weapons manufacture might just be the way they choose to operate.

If you can't find anything within your own borders, you'll have to look elsewhere, and this is when you can easily be bamboozled by the choice. You'll need to begin by defining what it is exactly that you want to do with your purchase. If you want a police weapon, for instance, you won't need the most rugged of rifles, as the gun will be stored in a clean, warm police armoury and not a muddy battlefield. Conversely, if you want to give your long-range recon troops the opportunity to disable enemy helicopters, there's no point in selecting a weapon that fires 5.56mm rounds, as they'll simply ricochet off a military vehicle's steel plating. Alternatively, if you want to provide each squad on patrol with the ability to stretch the range of their traditional assault rifles, but not necessarily to have a sniper who will act in a covert manner, then a semi-auto 'sniperised' assault rifle would be the ideal choice. (Indeed, the US Army did create such a creature to good effect with its Designated Marksman initiative.)

Once you've narrowed down the tactical role of the gun, you can start looking for possible suppliers. If you plan to buy 1,000 units, there's little point in contacting the small manufacturers who make specialised weapons to order, as they most likely won't be able to supply the number you require and they certainly will not be able to offer any acceptable form of support. Equally, if you contact a major manufacturer who has spent millions on developing a new gun, you should expect the price of his product to reflect his research and development costs!

Buyers realise very soon that there simply is no such thing as the ideal sniper rifle. There are many superb models that would be ideal in certain tactical situations, but there's no one model that can satisfy all needs. The temptation here might be to go for a standard assault rifle that will give you all the accuracy you could ever need and offers semi-automatic fire. However, such a weapon will almost certainly be calibred for a standard military rifle round, such as 5.56mm or 7.62mm, which, while being very lethal – especially the 7.62mm – will never have the long-range hitting power of the .338s of this world. These two standard rifle rounds – particularly the 5.56mm – are designed to be fired in bursts, or at least in quick succession, as one single round of either calibre might not hit a target with enough force to drop him.

Here's another interlude from Richard Brown:

I was stationed in Oman at the time when the Omani Army was switching from 7.62mm rifles to the 5.56mm Steyr AUG. During a firearms conversation with a British Army secondee, who was running a unit of soldiers known as '9 Squadron', I was told that, as part of the training regime with the new gun, the troops were being taught to fire two to three rounds where they had been shooting only one 7.62mm.

So why not make a semi-automatic in a hard-hitting, intermediary calibre, such as .338, to fill the market hole? Actually, a major player has; weapons manufacturer Barrett first unveiled its Model 98 at the Los Angeles Shot Show 1998. Even in 2005, however, not a single book we researched for this publication mentioned the gun. High-volume production is clearly not on the cards. Apparently, Barrett originally wanted to make a rifle that gave both bolt-action and semi-automatic capability. This idea was shelved for unknown reasons, although one possible explanation is that another bolt-action .338 would hardly have set the sniper-rifle world on fire.

The Barrett rifle is gas-operated, but its manufacturers obviously thought hard about the weapon before going into production as, interestingly, all of the gas mechanism is located behind the trigger mechanism, in the butt of the gun, which means that none of the sensitive harmonics of the barrel is affected when a round is discharged. The stock itself is polymer and has a bipod and folding stock. It weighs in at 7kg and is 117.5cm long.

But, of course, the key feature is that the gun offers a high-performance calibre in a semi-automatic package. Hard-hitting .50-calibre guns are common, but they're too big and cumbersome for many purposes and users. The .338 is a superb round and would benefit from being used in an even more assault-capable package. (Incidentally, the original Second World War Browning BAR is also made in .338 calibre, but this is a battlefield suppression weapon and not really designed for sniper use.)

Even as we sing the praises of the new Barrett, however, it's nevertheless important to reassert that there's still no single rifle that meets all the requirements for a sniper weapon. It's simply too broad a discipline. This section of the book, therefore, provides a snapshot of some of the world's great rifles. There's no bias here; we've simply included a broad selection of rifles that would fit all of the roles mentioned above, and we've been very careful not to put any emphasis on any one gun or operating method. This is a very small selection of guns, but it should give the reader a feel for the vast differences in rifles and how they work. Most of the guns mentioned here have several variants and are available in different calibres. Some are old and outdated, placed here for historical interest, while others represent the cutting edge of technology. Nevertheless, each is a lethal sniper rifle capable of one-shot kills at targets hundreds of metres away.

A Small Selection of Some of the World's Sniper Rifles

Steyr SSG (Austria)

The Austrian company Steyr-Daimler-Puch, who gave us the famous AUG assault rifle in 5.56mm, manufactures the SSG (ScharfShutzenGewehr) 69. As the name implies, the SSG 69 was accepted into Austrian Army Service in 1969. It's in .308 Winchester calibre, weighs 4.1kg and is 113cm long. It's a bolt-action gun with a rotating bolt and is fed from a removable box magazine, of which there are two varieties available, of five and ten rounds. There are also two different-sighted variants of the SSG, one with iron sights and one without. It comes with a 10x42 Hensoldt scope as standard.

The SSG offers all that one would expect from a sniper rifle, and in the late 1960s it was quite revolutionary. At that time, it performed very well against the competition in trials for a new American military sniper weapon, but it fell short of the others due to its expense.

The rifle was originally designed as a counter-sniper rifle, and therefore Steyr still make a variant that can be fitted with either a sound suppressor or a flash eliminator. It's a very slim weapon that looks its age when compared to the ergonomic modular design of the twenty-first century, but simplicity often works. The SSG rifle is a very accurate, simple and lightweight gun that performs very well.

PGM .338 (France)

The PGM rifle is a long-range weapon that can be used against both human and soft-skinned armour targets. The .338 is a superb round that offers a good balance in ballistic performance between the standard 7.62mm military bullet and the anti-matériel .50 BMG.

The PGM is an extremely odd-looking gun that on first sight might look very uncomfortable to use, its skeletal appearance not being to everyone's taste, but it's a fine weapon in operation, having been supplied to the French Army and selling well on the export market. The weapon looks odd only because its free-floating barrel is exposed, which makes it look fragile – which, of course, it isn't; the barrel is firmly fixed and benefits from all-round air circulation. Both compact and full-frame versions are available.

The PGM also comes as a fully equipped suppressor gun. This isn't a standard weapon with a fitted suppressor but a purpose-built silent gun, from much the same mould as the Heckler & Koch MP5SD series of sub-machine gun. The barrel is made by Walther and is externally fluted to minimise weight and improve heat dissipation. The business end of the gun also carries an effective muzzle brake, while its furniture (pistol grip and forearm) is made from polymer and is mounted on to the frame. With the .338 round, the guns can shoot accurately up to 1,200m.

Heckler & Koch MSG90 (Germany/UK)

The semi-automatic MSG 90 casts the perfect balance between the capacity of the standard infantry rifle and that of the sniper weapon. It's a robust rifle that can take both magazines of both five and twenty rounds. The gun has a Match-grade trigger that's the same unit as that on the manufacturer's flagship sniper rifle, the PSG1, while the barrel is cold-hammer forged and has a special harmonic stabiliser fitted to the muzzle end in order to give consistent barrel whip during firing.

Although the gun borrows its basic design from the G3 rifle, it is fully adjustable for the individual shooter. This similarity to the standard gun makes the transition for the prospective sniper easier and means that, while it doesn't provide full sniper capability, it can be used for long-range shooting if required.

Like the PSG1 (see below), the MSG 90 also features a silent bolt-closing device. Tactically, the rifle is different to the two already mentioned, as its semi-automatic mechanism ejects the spent cases. If the sniper wants to keep his location secret, he must therefore locate the empty case, which isn't easy if they're kicked 20 feet away.

Accuracy International L96A1 (UK)

In the early 1980s, the British Army finally realised that their ageing L42 Enfield sniper rifle was no longer a viable weapon. Although it had offered sterling service in the past, it was clear that there were simply better guns for the job out there. In 1986, therefore, they adopted the radical new Accuracy International rifle, which had been co-designed by Olympic shooter Malcolm Cooper. The polymer frame was at the time controversial, offering a plastic sleeve and a functional mechanism underneath. The British Army insisted on guaranteed hits at 600m, and the Accuracy can deliver superb groups (around 3 inches) at this range. The final version of the gun, which was 7.62mm in calibre and held a ten-round magazine, was designated the L96A1.

Today, Accuracy International make a variety of weapons, including an Arctic Warfare model that allows bolt operation in temperatures as low as minus 40 degrees Celsius, while the current British Army rifle is now the slightly modified L97A1, which is fitted as standard with a high-quality Schmidt & Bender 6x42 scope.

The current portfolio of Accuracy International includes a Super Magnum Arctic Warfare version in .338, which carries a weight-saving fluted barrel, while a police variant exists in either .243 Winchester Magnum or 7.62mm. There is also a pre-suppressed model and a .50 anti-matériel rifle which has a built-in anti-recoil system and an adjustable third supporting leg to help with precise aiming. It also folds up to make it easier to carry, but still weighs in at a sizeable 15kg. The sights have been mounted on a Picatinny rail, leaving the shooter free to use the scope of their choice.

Galil Sniper (Israel)

The Galil sniper rifle, discussed fully in chapter eleven, is one of the last remaining sniper rifles in the world that differs very little from the infantry model on which it is based. It's chambered in 7.62mm and can be fitted with a scope, while the fully automatic mode on its parent standard rifle has been removed. The Galil sniper rifle is really more of a marksman gun that would be carried in the squad and shouldn't be confused with assault-rifle-style weapons such as the MSG90 (see above), which is a purpose-built sniper rifle. The Galil really is just an accurised infantry gun, but, as discussed in chapter eleven, it fits in well with Israeli military doctrine. The only real glitch with the gun is that it weighs in at an uncomfortable 8kg.

CV-98/99 (Russia)

The CV-98 is the new Russian sniper rifle that will eventually replace the venerated Dragunov. Calibred in 7.65 (NATO, not the Kalashnikov 7.62mmx39), it's advertised as a designated sniper rifle that can destroy moving and 'masked' targets as well as the more traditional sniper targets. It has a ten-round magazine capacity with a bolt-action mechanism offering a ten-round-per-minute aim-and-shoot time. The gun hails from the Izhmash factory, which has churned out a mind-boggling number of AK47s in its time. For a Russian gun, the CV-98 actually looks quite modern; while some of the design is surely cribbed from its predecessors, it at least shrugs off the old Kalashnikov appearance of the Dragunov.

The sister weapon to the CV-98 is the CV-99. This rifle – which breaks down into a worryingly small suitcase – is chambered in a radical 5.6mm rimfire cartridge and is definitely manufactured with the special-operations community in mind. Like the Accuracy International guns, the CV-99 has a sporting heritage, its design deriving from the Biathlon 7-2 sporting rifle. It features an odd crank-operated locking mechanism that makes very rapid bolt-action fire possible and comes with a sound suppressor fitted as standard, while the butt carries two spare five-round magazines. Finally, it's possible to remove the butt completely and replace it with a pistol grip.

Walther WA2000 (Germany)

The .300-calibre Walther made a brief appearance in the opening sequence of the James Bond film *The Living Daylights*. It has a radical design, even by today's standards, and on its introduction in 1981 it was hailed as signifying the future of sniper rifles, primarily due to the good breeding of Walther weaponry and its space-age design. The WA2000 has a bullpup design (i.e. the magazine is stored behind the trigger, as with the SA80 and Steyr AUG assault rifles, and in anticipation of large sales to the law-enforcement market Walther also offered optional chambering for 7.62mm NATO (.308 Winchester) and 7.5mm Swiss (they knew that the gun wasn't robust enough to cut it in the military market but that it might just catch the attention of the world's police forces). Unfortunately, like so many radical ideas, the WA2000 came with a serious price tag – too steep for most budgets – and mass-production was never realised. It will always be a fascinating weapon, albeit never for the right reasons.

Barrett .50BMG (USA)

The .50BMG was the first modern large-calibre sniper rifle, and

300 units were sold initially to the US military prior to the first Gulf War, its manufacturers boasting its ability to produce a confirmed kill at 1,800m. Indeed, the stopping power of the round is legendary and struck fear into the heart of the British Army in Ireland when it was confirmed that a soldier had been killed by one, rendering obsolete overnight British Army-issue body armour.

The Barrett is often called the 'Light Fifty', which is something of a misnomer considering that the gun weighs nearly 13kg, and it immediately set the benchmark for later guns, such as the aforementioned Accuracy International .50. Its hard long-range punch made it ideal for anti-matériel use, such as against communications systems and sensitive parts of distant vehicles, though it can also be used to detonate (at a safe distance) unexploded ordnance and mines. It carries ten rounds in a huge magazine and has a muzzle velocity of 850m per second.

US M21 (USA)

Built on the trusted frame of the M14 rifle, the M21 saw extensive service in Vietnam and later conflicts. It's an accurised version of the M14 in NATO-standard 7.62mm, weighs 7.2kg and has the benefit of being semi-automatic fire with a twenty-round box. However, although the M21 closely resembles the M14, it is fundamentally a new gun, using only selected barrels and a trigger mechanism hand-assembled by gunsmiths. Its gas-operated system – a key feature in the original M14 – has also been re-engineered for smooth operation and the gun is typically equipped with a 3x–9x-zoom scope. The traditional wooden stock of the M14 gun was deemed unsuitable for sniper use and so, while the shape was retained, the stock of the M21 is made of a composite of wood and impregnated polymer to create an individual product.

Armament Technology AT1-M24
Type 1 And 2 (USA)

Although one of the small players who now really only focus on manufacturing sights, AT are worth a mention as they are – or were – living proof that, no matter how good you think your product is, there's always a way to improve it. They took the US Army M24 rifle and gave it an upgrade to produce a weapon capable of stunning accuracy.

The exact twist of the rifling produced by AT is the key to their success, while the stock is reinforced with Kevlar and aircraft-grade aluminium is used in the mechanism's manufacture. The Type 1 has a fixed stock while the Type 2 is adjustable. The rifle sold to both the serious sportsman and the law-enforcement community in the US.

DPMS AR-15 Variants (USA)

DPMS guns are worthy of inclusion, as they're appearing increasingly often in the hands of semi-snipers – that is, typically members of the police who require sharpshooting capabilities, rather than the classic sniper who hides in wait for his prey. DPMS rifles all look fairly similar, something like an M16 that has been massively reworked, but there the similarity stops. However, it does give the shooter the advantage of having a rifle with which he is probably familiar, and it will also accept a number of M16 style bolt-ons. All DPMS rifles are calibred for .223 (which is really 5.56mm by another name), which really then knocks them out of the true snipe-rifle category, although had John Allen Muhammad had one of these rather than his Bushmaster – which, to the untrained eye, looks almost identical – then the Montgomery County Police Department in Washington would have had much more trouble, as his effective range would have been greatly increased.

All DPMS rifles have lost their trademark carry handle, which identified them with the M16, instead bearing a sight rail, such as a Picatinny. They are all of a high quality internally and are capable of taking a bipod, while their barrels are Match-grade. Indeed, DPMS have a unique manufacturing process whereby the new barrels are cooled to a frigid minus 180 degrees centigrade for up to thirty hours, then heated to a searingly high temperature and allowed to cool to produce hardened steel of the highest quality.

Depending on the particular model, DPMS guns weigh in at around 4–5kg and are all semi-automatic, being ideally suited to squad marksmen and police sharpshooters. As the bulk of the fore end and stock is polymer, they can be produced in a variety of colours, from white to sand.

Heckler & Koch PSG1 (Germany/UK)

The PSG1 is a purpose-built police rifle. It's a heavy (8kg) 7.62mm weapon that can be fired not only from its high-quality bipod but also from a precision tripod rest, which can be purchased with the weapon. The weight of the gun means that it's not best suited to being carried around a battlefield, although it's very at home during urban shooting or in a position where it can be mounted for long periods. It has a bull barrel and hand-worked mechanism and trigger unit. Like its sibling the MSG90, the PSG1 can fire only semi-automatic rounds and has a bolt-closing device that can offer the shooter silent loading. A unique feature of the PSG1 is that its sight mounts are permanently moulded on to the top of the receiver, thus removing at least one way that the sight could move off zero. The gun comes with a contoured wooden grip, although this can be replaced with one of polymer if desired.

Harris Gunworks (USA)

Harris make a wide variety of rifles for all purposes, though they are all military weapons, through and through. The company has divided its product range into two categories: classic sniper weapons, which will offer good accuracy up to 800m; and heavy rifles (normally in .50BMG calibre), which can fire up to an astonishing 1,500m.

The Phoenix rifle is available in .300 Phoenix and .30 Magnum calibres. It's one of several 'traditional'-style rifles made by Harris, but even so it's a high-tech, modern weapon with a fibreglass stock and matt coating.

It's in .50-calibre territory, however, that Harris really become a unique manufacturer of defence equipment. Unlike most sniper-rifle manufacturers who sport a single .50-calibre model in their range, Harris have several products. One of these, the M-92 Bullpup Long Range rifle, is an unusual (i.e. ugly), squat weapon that takes the form of an anti-matériel gun. It is short for a .50 BMG gun, being only 105cm long (the Accuracy International is 118cm), yet it can deliver a .50 round accurately up to 1,500m.

Still believing that there was more accuracy to be had with a .50 bullet, Harris then developed the M-96 Long Range Sniper rifle, which is a huge weapon, not just in its 143cm length but also in its general bulk. The massive muzzle brake at the end of the gun gives a clue to the performance that the manufacturers are expecting. The M-96 is a semi-automatic weapon with a five-round capacity and a 74cm-long barrel (compare this to Accuracy's 65cm barrel), weighing in at over 11kg, and is capable of delivering a hard-hitting round up to 2,000m.

Lee-Enfield No. 4 (T) (UK)

As mentioned elsewhere in this book, the Lee-Enfield No. 4 (T) was the standard sniper rifle of the British Army during the Second World War and was, in fact, simply the Lee-Enfield No. 4

weapon that had above-average accuracy, which was then equipped with a 3x scope and a cheek piece (hastily screwed into the butt) to give correct scope/eye relief. By all accounts, they were good weapons – which is unsurprising, as they inherited the characteristics of what's regarded as one of the best fighting rifles of all times. The .303 round wasn't particularly ideal for sniping, but its performance was well known to the users of the new gun and it was readily available. Even with the scope, the gun weighed in at less than 5.5kg.

Erma SR-100 (Germany)

Erma is a name steeped in history. It was the Erma factory that produced the MP40 (Schmeisser) sub-machine gun, and this feat alone ensures the company a place in history. In later years, the name became synonymous with low-cost classic-design handguns.

When the Erma SR-100 rifle was unveiled, it was a radical departure from their previous product list. It's a super-expensive rifle that has firmly taken its place at the top end of the market. Like the PSG1, it was designed with an eye to law-enforcement communities as well as elite counter-terrorist units.

The ER-100, meanwhile, is a bolt-action, magazine-fed rifle with a barrel that can be changed quickly, allowing for rechambering in .308 Winchester (7.62 x51mm NATO), .300 Winchester Magnum and .338 Lapua Magnum. Calibres can be swapped on one rifle in the matter of minutes by replacing the barrel, bolt and magazine, while the lock on its free-floating barrel has been patented. At under 7kg with scope, the gun is relatively light.

Remington 700 (USA)

The Remington model 700 Police is a repackaged Remington model 700 VS, which is a hunting gun used by civilians. The company has been making this fine weapon since 1962, and today it's widely used by too many police authorities in the US to mention.

In 1967, the first of these rifles, fitted with Redfield scopes, arrived in Vietnam. They performed well in the hot environment, and their lightness (just 4kg without scope) made them easy to carry around. The rifle's original wooden stock was kept for many years, but it has now been replaced by one of polymer. The weapon can still be seen in the hands of US Marines today.

Robar (USA)

The company Robar was established by a keen hunter, Robert Barrkman, and was originally a custom shop but soon began to produce high-quality sniper rifles, using the Remington 700 as a basic framework. Their weapons are made to order, to the point at which some models don't have specified calibres; the user chooses his own. Some of their rifles are short, such as the QR2 (Quick Reaction). This gun has a fluted barrel and is guaranteed to deliver a half-inch group at 100m – a high degree of accuracy – while stocks are manufactured by the globally renowned company McMillan. Taking full advantage of current computer technology to impregnate colours into the plastic, Robar offer their weapons in just about any camouflage option to match the Disruptive Pattern Material (DPM) of the environment in which they'll be used, and desert, woodland, jungle and urban colours are all available. Some models have a collapsible stock, which makes transportation easy, and some of their smaller-calibre guns are light, the SR90 .308 weighing in at just 4.7kg.

Mauser 98K (Germany)

This weapon served as the backbone of the German Army in the Second World War. The Mauser 98K was made in huge numbers and many still exist in refurbished condition in Eastern Europe and South America.

Like the Lee-Enfield, the sniper variant of this bolt-action rifle kept the original 7.92mm bullet and woodwork. It had a five-round magazine and, due to the good locking action of the bolt, it lent itself well to sniping. Highly accurate models were selected from normal stock, their mechanisms were tuned and they were then topped off with a 4x scope from Zeiss or, possibly, Hensoldt (both are now very expensive and highly regarded scopes). Like so many of its competitors, the Mauser 98K was a wartime weapon that was little upgraded from the standard gun; it just gave a good shooter the chance to bleed more accurate distance from each high-velocity round. One major advantage for the gun was that it weighed only 3.9kg, which made it very easy to hold on target.

On **The Way To Dixie** – **A** Short Story

The following short story was an exercise in creative writing I set myself whilst reaserching this book with Richard.

Certain pieces of historical data appealed to me, so I decided to do more digging in those general fields and uncovered much information, which although didn't naturally fit into the constraints of the individual chapters, could inspire a piece of short fiction, thus showing how research/fact can be applied to fiction and, furthermore, provide a little light entertainment at the end of this book. We sincerely hope you enjoy the diversion. *CC*

Colonel Anthony Creighton of the Royal Scots Guards (Rtd) was an old hand at exhibitions. Always well presented, spit-and-polish and just a genial use of levity. It was an act he savoured, but rarely, in his autumn years, cherished. The bones creaked a little more these days and the smile always cracked his cheeks; he was now so unused to such activity. But he considered himself a staunch patriot, true to traditional values and aristocracy, so he had to attend such an exhibition as the NRA – not because firearms were involved, but because her gracious majesty Queen Victoria was to be in attendance.

He wondered how long it was since he'd last been in Wimbledon. Ten, fifteen years maybe? Yes, that would be about right. Visiting a wine merchant. He'd bought an excellent hock. Well, several cases, in truth. Drunk the lot about... well, ten to fifteen years ago, actually.

Creighton tugged at his spotless tunic and took a deep breath. Oh yes, such male elegance, even at fifty-five. The Queen would be impressed, for sure.

Florence entered the room, her elegant gown simply billowing. 'Oh, do say you're ready, Creighton!' She always used his surname, something of the military manner brushing off on her.

'But of course, my dear, but of course,' Creighton replied, waxing his immodest moustache.

'You're such a bore when one is getting ready,' Florence added.

'Only because I can't tell you how wonderful you look through your laborious costume changes.'

'Oh, do say you like it, Anthony?' Likewise, she always used his first name when seeking approval.

'An absolute disaster, my dear.'

'Thank you. An agonising thirty minutes and three maids to assist.'

'How tiresome, my dear. You simply suffer for your art. I would kiss you now but you may get waxed, so let us at least repair to our carriage.'

'We're not late, are we?'

'Oh God, no. Not with her majesty in attendance. No, politely tardy, I'm sure. Come along now.'

And together, as always, the two socialites went on their way to

Wimbledon, for there was little else they wished to do with their lives.

As they trundled along the uneven road from their country retreat in Bexley (opposite one of the quaintest churches you would ever wish to see in spitting distance of London), Creighton began to speculate on the patrons of the exhibition.

'I wonder if Mr Dickens will be in attendance.'

'I rather doubt it, dear,' Florence replied with only a passing interest. 'He seems such a recluse nowadays.'

'Nonsense. His public readings are most popular.'

'Indeed,' Florence said tartly. 'If one wishes to spend one's time in the company of bounders and bores, then I suppose one must continue to feed one's ego.'

'Oh, really?' Creighton replied mischievously.

'Now there's no need to be offensive, Creighton.'

'Oh, come on. You can be such a hag at times, I'm surprised that I ever picked you up off the shelf.'

'You did it for your own good. And I stand by my comment concerning Mr Dickens. He alienates himself from society deliberately to inflate his ego in front of the lower classes, and that is simply unacceptable.'

'I believe her majesty applauds him for such action.'

'And I suppose you do, too?'

'It doesn't wound me as much as you. I have served with bounders and bores, as you call them, and quite frankly they certainly move with a bayonet up their rear ends.'

'Really, Creighton! You astonish me.'

'It astonishes them too, my dear. No, no, I don't think we'll see Mr Dickens today.'

'Thank God for that. I do believe you would engage with him.'

'Quite possibly. He is practically a neighbour now, you know?

Moved to Gad's Hill Place, Higham, a month or so ago. And, indeed, his latest work is much praised.'

'About the lower classes, I'm sure,' Florence said with disdain.

'About a boy who grows to manhood and finds his legacy in an escaped convict.'

'I retire to Bedlam. What rot! Escaped convict? How inappropriate.'

'*Great Expectations*.'

'They certainly must be,' Florence said with a haughty laugh.

'That's the name of the book, Florence. Oh, do please keep up.'

'I shall keep up when I choose, Creighton, and not a second sooner. How can one be entertained on such uneven ground?'

'Yes, I must have a word with the driver.'

'Well I hope you shall, the seat is playing absolute murders with my complaint, as well you know.'

It is best here to leave the couple to attend to their travel conditions in peace and move on approximately an hour, to Wimbledon and the NRA exhibition, a gala occasion if there ever was one. The finest of the glitterati were in attendance, with the finest of botanical excellence in either headgear or pots dotted around what would otherwise be an almost bare space.

'What a centrepiece, Gerald. An absolute monster of a contraption. Do you think her majesty will actually shoot the gun?'

'Of course she will. Especially when she knows she is guaranteed a bullseye. It will simply be the highlight of the show, Peepee.' Gerald then burst into hysterics, a loud, horsy crow that forced him to adjust his monocle several times.

Peepee – or, rather, Percival Perlhampton – lost interest in the maniac and decided to find somebody beautiful to speak to. It didn't take long.

'Lady Eves, how wonderful to see you.' He stooped to kiss the ivory hand of the doll-like figure that stood before him.

The sumptuous nineteen-year-old flushed slightly and said with just too much theatricality, 'I am *far* too early not to be desperate.'

'Well, you would make a Perlhampton simply flattered if you would engage in some light conversation.'

Lady Eves laughed too loudly at the compliment, but Perlhampton ignored her impetuosity; he needed to, because he was twenty years her senior. 'Have you been to the Crystal Palace recently?'

'Of course, Percival. The cuisine is simply divine. Have you partaken?'

'But of course, my dear. It's absolutely delightful.'

Lady Eves's laughter rocked the most delicate of flowers nearby, but they were unnoticed by Colonel Anthony Creighton (Rtd), who smartly and most confidently entered the fray, Florence a submissive and genteel second.

'Creighton!' a cannon-fire bark. It was General Saunderson.

'Sir! Marvellous to see you,' Creighton roared.

Florence busied herself with the ladies at the table.

The general lowered his voice. 'Have you seen the new Whitworth Sharpshooter rifle?'

'No, not yet, sir. Just arrived.'

'Acquaint yourself, man. Acquaint, I say! Excellent piece of machinery. Suits me, man. I say, it suits me.'

'But sir, a general and a rifle?'

'Oh, I know what you're saying – a scary prospect. But you must keep your hand in, you know? I mean, look at the National Rifle Association's free-for-all. People coming from all over the land to shoot off up to 1,000 yards. That's Oxford Circus to Tottenham Court Road. Unheard of. Well, unless you got the Whitworth, my boy, unless you've got the Whitworth, eh?'

'But do they manufacture in Britain?'

'They damn well will. Too good not to. Well, leave that little detail to me. Did you know that the Queen put up a £250 prize for the NRA shoot-out? Not bad, eh? Eh?'

'Sir, but Whitworth? Surely American?'

'Creighton, you and I get along, don't we?'

'Yes, of course sir.'

'We understand each other. Traditionalists and all that, eh? Eh?'

'Without question. Where would I be without high tea and fox hunting?'

Both men laughed heartily, 'Oh yes, Creighton, where would the world be without either, eh?'

'Let us not fool each other, sir. The extinction of such pleasurable pastimes would never happen.'

'Oh, absolutely not. Not in out lifetimes, anyway. But I am concerned, Creighton. Yes, quite concerned. Do you feel that values are going to the wall?'

'They have been doing so since my grandfather's time, sir.'

'You don't have to go back that far. My father was at Waterloo. Nothing like that nowadays, nothing to pump the heart to capacity like a good old-fashioned battle. Give me the bad odds at Bosworth Field and I'll turn strategy into an art form. Well, you know where King Richard went wrong, don't you...'

The general, to Creighton's delight, had no time to engage in further pleasantries. Her majesty had arrived and a vast audience had quickly assembled to greet her.

Florence came to Creighton's side and Lady Saunderson to the general's as the Queen was most graciously offered entrance.

'Doesn't she look splendid?' Florence whispered.

'Didn't I tell you that you were a hag, my dear?' Creighton chided. The good lady Florence gently elbowed him in the stomach.

'Good job I'm wearing my corset,' Creighton managed to say before a bombastic theatrical called for their ears, handkerchief in hand and feigning tears.

The gentlemen's chests inflated with pride whilst the women doffed their heads and became – or, in Florence's case, attempted to look – genteel.

Her gracious majesty Queen Victoria had been positioned in front of (actually, a safe distance away from) a crazy-looking contraption that held the Whitworth Sharpshooter.

'That's the gun, my boy,' the general growled.

To Creighton's trained eye, it didn't look much different from any other rifle, but he was aware that the secret to the gun's accuracy was its uniquely twisted hexagonal barrel.

'And now,' the bombast cried, 'her gracious majesty Queen Victoria has kindly consented to fire the Whitworth Sharpshooter rifle.'

There was a painfully long pause while one end of a silk thread was tied to the trigger of the gun and the other end offered to the Queen. No one dared say a word, but Creighton could work out what was going on. The weird-looking contraption in which the gun rested snugly had been positioned in such a way that, when fired, the bullet would hit the bullseye of a target 100m away.

Her majesty graciously pulled the trigger, the gun roared and both rifle and queen momentarily disappeared in a cloud of white smoke. The rangemaster first ensured that her majesty was still in good health and then signalled for the target to be assessed. A young lad appeared out from the butts and, with much reverence, declared a bull. There was a tremendous flood of applause, and someone in the background breathed a sigh of relief – probably Mr Whitworth himself, Creighton thought.

When the formalities of the royal occasion were over and the Queen was safely on her way back to London, General

Saunderson took Creighton to one side and draped his arm over his shoulder. 'Now listen, Creighton. I'm going to let you in on a little secret. I'm going to back Whitworth to obtain a British manufacturing base within the next two years. When he does, you and I will have a little game to play.'

'Really, sir? And what's that?'

'Gun-running, dear boy. Gun-running.'

'Gun-running? Oh, jolly good. But to who?'

'To our American cousins over the pond, of course.'

'Oh yes. But we're not really flavour of the month – any month – over there, are we?'

'Ah, but we will be, dear boy, we will be. There are tensions brewing. Some say civil war – north versus south. You see, the aristocratic southerners are getting their land destroyed, everything they've worked hard to protect. My brother is one such landowner, and we must really protect our interests in the south because they instil British values, dear boy, and not many people do that nowadays. Shoulder to shoulder, my boy, shoulder to shoulder – the British aristocracy and the Confederates.'

'Well, sir, it sounds like fun. When do we start?'

'Oh, I'll be in touch in about a year or two. Now, let us celebrate our union and charge some glasses.'

'At least several glasses, sir, I trust?'

'Absolutely, dear boy, absolutely. A man who doesn't take the drink is *not* to be trusted under any circumstance, do you hear me? Any circumstance. Now, where's the blasted drinks?' Saunderson moved away, mumbling about the 'dashed ineptitude we didn't toast the Queen'.

During the next couple of years, Creighton was rather hopeful that the general would forget their little chat, but then decided that nothing could possibly come of the gun-running idea – it was surely too weird and wonderful – and so, stupidly, stopped worrying.

Then, in July 1862, disaster struck when General Saunderson turned up unannounced on his doorstep. Creighton had been reading the latest edition of *Household Words* when the door was nearly thumped in. Obviously, the butler was keen to open the door quickly, and Creighton waited in his lounge to receive his persistent guest. He was slightly taken aback to see the general turn up, not unlike Rumpelstiltskin requesting the Queen's baby.

The general spread his hands. 'And here I am,' he said continuing a two-year-old conversation as if they'd last spoken only two minutes ago.

Creighton gulped. 'Well, I say. You haven't done it, have you, sir?'

'Done it, dear boy? Done it? My God, we're selling guns like hot cakes from deepest, darkest Manchester. What's more, I've chartered a ship, and you and I, my friend, *you and I*, are off to Dixie.'

'And who is she?'

'Hang it all, Creighton! It's a place in southern America, land of our cousins – well, my brother. A couple of hundred guns his way should see him through. What fun, eh? Eh? What fun, I say.'

'Yes. And frightfully dangerous, too, I should say, sir.'

'Oh, just a little. May get trouble from that Union lot. They may try and scuttle us, take the guns or grab a bounty on the ship, but we can fight, can't we, Creighton? We can fight! Show the strength of the British Empire. What are the Union lot, anyway? They're riff-raff, that's what they are. What do you say? Not pulling out on me now, are you?'

'No, sir, not at all. I simply thought that, if we were going to face some trouble, I'd better take the wife.'

'Excellent idea, Creighton! I'll bring mine, too. We can't have too much fun then, can we? Need the women to keep us in line.'

'I wasn't thinking that at all, sir. I simply thought of throwing her over the side in shark-infested waters, that's all.'

'You may have a point there,' the general enthused a little too seriously. 'But I take your point,' he said at last. 'The women could come in handy. Washing, cooking, sewing, all those things that take us away from the real business: shooting. We'll have such fun. Put some targets in the rigging and away we go.'

Creighton cracked a smile. 'It jolly well does too, sir. It jolly well does too, I say! When do we sail?'

'Oh, not for a month yet, but you must come to the factory and try out the Whitworth Sharpshooter rifle first. See what you're getting yourself into and all that.'

'I look forward to it, sir,' Creighton said.

The general moved towards the door. 'I'll send you a formal invitation to attend the factory. I'll be in touch soon. We'll whip those Union boys in a well-trained British military manner.'

'Excellent, sir. Thank you. I'll look forward to it.'

'So will I, dear boy. So will I.' And as quickly as he'd arrived, the general was gone.

Florence glided into the room. 'Really, if the general has to turn up unannounced, he must really speak more quietly. I deliberately heard every word. So very kind of you to think of me, darling.' She kissed Creighton on each cheek.

'Well, I thought a bit of peril might do us good,' Creighton said.

'Taking the sea air is what appeals to me most. I was born in Bournemouth, you know.'

'Well, I forgive you that. You get a better class of person in Aldershot.'

'It isn't that far away, Creighton.'

'Far enough, dear.'

The month passed slowly as only it could in a sleepy village like Bexley. The sun shone brightly each day and copious amounts of wine were drunk. Wasn't retirement great fun? Not really. Once a soldier, always a soldier, and Creighton did nothing but dream of pistol, cold steel and rifle. God, he had to be severely out of practice.

The following month, he found out exactly how badly out of practice he was in the backyard of the Whitworth factory in Sackville Street, Manchester.

'Dear God!' General Saunderson declared. 'Well, I'm pleased you were never protecting my flank. Hang it all, it's only 150 yards!'

'Not cutting the mustard at the moment, sir,' Creighton confessed.

'I do believe you're splitting the fence on the way,' the general observed. 'How the deuce are we going to protect ourselves if our ship is boarded, eh? We'll be the laughing stock of... of...'

'The English Channel?' Creighton offered.

'Well, it's not going to be English much longer with shooting like that, is it?'

'With all due respect, sir, are you any better?'

'Well, of course I am! I've been practising like mad the past month. I take it you've been sunning yourself in the lap of luxury, damn you. It could cost us our lives and those blasted wives of ours, too.'

'Don't say that too loudly sir. They may...' But Creighton didn't have time to warrant his fears.

Florence and Lady Saunderson stood in the doorway. 'I think you should let us shoot,' Lady Saunderson observed.

'Why should you boys have all the fun?' Florence added. 'Besides, I'm sure we can knock spots of you two, couldn't we, Margaret?'

'Choose your weapons, gentlemen. The cavalry has arrived!'

The men went for their rifles; the ladies unveiled a pair of Colt Navy .36 Percussion revolvers.

'Where did you get those from?' Creighton exclaimed.

'I say, aren't they from our armoury, Margaret?' the general asked.

'Indeed they are. You don't expect a lady to bruise her shoulder with a cumbersome thing like that, do you?' said Margaret, nodding at her husband's weapon. 'The .36 is quite civilised to shoot.'

'I wouldn't say that they're the first thing in elegance, my dear.'

'Well, let's see, shall we?'

Creighton noted the general's gulp, but after the first two rounds were fired at the 30-yard pistol target from each of the women, he was gulping himself. 'Florence, I demand you to tell me where you learned to shoot like that! You're positively indecently accurate with a pistol.'

'A woman's touch,' Lady Saunderson said.

'If you must know, it was Lady Saunderson who taught me,' confessed Florence airily.

'When?' Creighton demanded with a shrill edge.

'When you were sun-worshipping in the garden, dear husband.'

'Dash it all! What did I accuse you of doing?' the general roared.

More out of embarrassment than anything else, Creighton reloaded, took his stance, made aim and took a shot at the 150-yard rifle target. He split the centre ring.

'I say, that was quite impressive,' the general said. 'Don't tell me, you're only a good shot when angry. I once knew a chap like that. Damned good fellow. Got shot to bits in India.'

'I intend to keep alive, thank you. Anyway, long-range shooting isn't my thing. I like to see the whites of their eyes.'

'Hm. You'd probably never fire a shot in India, then. Most of them have bloodshot eyes. It's the dust, you know.'

Creighton didn't really know if the general was joking or not, but suddenly the rifle was taken out of his hand and the general was ushering him into the building.

'They're cowards Florence,' Lady Saunderson called out behind them.

'Bad losers, more like,' Florence replied.

'Well, in that case, we'll just have to challenge each other. Come on, now.'

General Saunderson found a quiet room but nevertheless spoke in a hushed voice to Creighton. 'Now listen, Creighton. After what's just happened, I'm going to come clean with you. Firstly, yes, we are gun-running to Dixie. The guns are for my brother – none of that has changed – but I do have an ulterior motive.

'I want to train the best shooters in the Confederate Army to shoot at distance and, as far as I'm concerned, this new rifle is the best weapon for doing so. I don't just want to gun-run and have jolly good fun. Well, actually, that does come into it. But I want to train a crack troop of lads in the art of long-range shooting. It's never been done before, and I dare say the Unionists won't know what hit them.

'I – *we* – can give my brother and his army the upper hand by applying a little bit of lateral thinking to their plight. One problem, though: we need to work out some drill exercises when we're aboard ship. Nothing could be simpler. Climb the rigging, shoot a tiny target across the deck; lie almost hidden in the crosstrees and shoot a lantern in the far corner of the stern. These are skills that can be learned, Creighton. They can be learned by you and I on an unsteady ship, and they can be learned by the best marksmen in the Confederate Army. What do you think?'

'I think we're all bloody mad.'

'But?'

'But yes, I'll do it. It sounds an interesting concept, because all the soldier has to do is enter a wooded area, unseen, and wait for the enemy to rear its head and then *boom!* All over.'

'Well, they can always wait up in the trees, heavily camouflaged with foliage, and allow the enemy to get closer.'

'It appears, on the face of it, to be a cowardly way of going into battle.'

'That's the whole point. Doing it this way, you don't *have* to go into battle. You're lying in wait on the way to the battlefield. Everything's fair in love and war, you know. Survival of the fittest, and the most intelligent. We're fighting with our minds, not just our spirits. Do you see where I'm coming from? I'm talking about saving people's lives here.'

Creighton thought he was talking about taking people's lives, not saving them, but thought it unwise to interrupt.

The general had, however, finished his little speech. 'What do you think?' he prompted.

'The concept is pretty sound, I'm sure. I also like the idea of practising on the way out. But there seems such a lot to do still.'

'Not at all, dear boy. I've already chartered a ship from Liverpool as I've already told you. We sail in seven days.'

'What? But that's preposterous!'

'No it's not,' said Florence, who was now standing in the doorway with Lady Saunderson. 'I've known about it all month. Our baggage is already in Liverpool.'

Creighton could only gape in response. He wasn't used to this at all. It seemed that everyone had the upper hand on him this time.

'I think we'd better get some extra practice in, don't you?' said the general. 'Not because of the Unionists – good lord, no; so that we can take on these dratted women and, by all the gods, win!'

As it turned out, the men did win, although the women accused them of cheating and moved the target back 50 yards after each shot. Ten shots each at an eventual distance of 650 yards became a true marksman's sport. Unfortunately, no one hit a bull at such a distance; Creighton managed one only at 350 yards and only the general and Lady Saunderson at 300 yards.

In conclusion, the two couples decided that the shooting match had been jolly good fun, but the general left in a rather thoughtful mood, evidently plotting a sharpshooting skills course. Creighton initially felt that the long-shooter idea was a good one, but then had second thoughts. The soldier couldn't go running into battle and then suddenly go down on one knee and shoot from distance. He'd kill his comrades running past him!

But that wasn't what the general was referring to, was it? He wanted the shooter to hide in shadows to pinpoint the enemy without them knowing and then, when their guard was down, kill them. Surely, though, that tactic was only good for one shot? Actually, maybe not if the sharpshooter was well hidden. Camouflaged.

Yes, the general's idea was starting to sound interesting. They could practise while travelling down to Dixie, then pour their enthusiasm on the general's brother and the Confederates. If such a manoeuvre proved successful, they could come home with the positive experience and transform the British Army! Now that was worth coming out of retirement for.

To both the Saundersons and the Creightons, there was no risk. This was a holiday, a bit of fun, yet at the same time it was something to get their teeth into – an adventure. But when the HMS *Cloud* sailed out of port a week later, Creighton watched the mainland for hours as the ship moved down and away from Britain and her marvellous pretensions. With his gaze fixed on the receding shore, Creighton's bravado wasn't so fierce, and for some reason he couldn't puff his chest out as much as he felt he ought.

'What on earth are you doing?' Florence announced. 'You look like a robin gasping for air.'

Creighton was startled but quickly recovered. It was never good to expose one's weaknesses to one's wife; Florence would only use the tactic again one day if she felt it worked.

'Taking the sea air,' Creighton recovered. 'Filling the blood with salt. It's so bracing.'

'Anthony, it is not bracing, it is positively freezing. Now come below before you catch your death of cold. A tot of rum does wonders, I've just discovered.'

'My God, I'm going to lose you to a gin alley,' Creighton exclaimed.

'Nothing of the kind,' General Saunderson declared, taking to the deck with two Whitworth rifles and a noggin of rum for Creighton. 'Get that down you quickly, man,' he said, proffering the rum, 'and then your good lady can take the empty vessel below and keep well away whilst we start our business.'

Creighton was in no mood to argue; he was feeling the cold quite horribly. Although he wore a long, heavy coat, the chill had definitely found a way inside. He sank the rum in one hit, his face instantly glowing red and his eyes watering, but he refused to cough or splutter; that was no way for a gentleman to behave, especially a gentleman of the sea.

Florence took the empty noggin below. Now the only people on deck were Creighton and the five hands that the general had hired: the captain, the navigator, the first mate and two able-bodied seamen. The general dismissed the two seamen and left the other three to their duties on the quarterdeck. 'Please don't move from your position; you might get yourselves killed, and that would be most troubling for those that survive,' the general said in his most sarcastic tone.

Creighton could see that the captain despised the general, but he knew that this was simply because the general called the shots – and paid the wages – when normally that privilege would fall to the captain alone. But if Creighton knew the general well – and he believed he did – then the captain and his crew had been paid handsomely for this voyage. There was no question of mutiny.

The general instantly got to work. 'Right. Take one of these, Creighton.' He handed him a rifle. 'Have you got the powder, ball and caps?'

'Yes, sir. In my pocket.'

'Right. Good. Now I want you to climb the rigging and get into the crosstrees. I want you to make yourself comfortable up there and then, in one shot – and I mean one shot – I want you to hit the bucket on the poop deck.'

'You are joking, sir!'

'Never more serious in my life. You see, Creighton, what we want to achieve here is a level of accuracy in poor conditions – cold, height, relatively cramped shooting position – a level of skill our enemy cannot come anywhere near. Do you understand?'

'Yes, I do, but I could get killed up there. My hands are freezing, and I'm not a sailor.'

'You do realise, if you spoke to me on the parade ground like that, I would have you shot at dawn? But as you are almost an equal on this assignment – and I stress the "almost" – I'll overlook your insubordination.

'Listen to me, man! There's more to this than meets the eye. What we need to do is create a troop of men who are in their prime. Fighting fit. The best. They know the area they are to work in – or, at least, they've trained in extreme conditions and so know and can adapt to things when they don't know the territory. They are fearless and expert with the Whitworth Sharpshooter *as the preferred weapon*. Do you see where I'm coming from? We are going to form an elite. A new army!'

The hairs began to rise on the back of Creighton's neck and, with a new determination, he started to climb the rigging. The general was right.

'That's my boy!' the general shouted.

But as the chill wind became increasingly violent as he ascended, Creighton didn't hear a word the general said. All he could feel was the butt of the rifle swaying under his backside and his hands growing numb. As he reached the crosstrees, he could feel the fragility of the ship under him, the way the ocean pushed it almost haphazardly onwards through her convex shoulders, squeezing the heart of oak and sending a shivering pulse up towards its extremities at the topmast. *So this is what 'shiver me timbers' means*, Creighton thought almost hysterically.

There was no going back now. His coat, although it protected him from the most awful biting chill of the wind, was cumbersome, restricting his movements. However, he reached his goal, pushing along the crosstrees and hooking himself into a tight position, wrapping a foot around the wood that supported him so far above the deck.

Creighton unslung his rifle and prepared it, fumbling in his pockets for the few lead balls and percussion caps he'd brought with him. Despite the cold, he was sweating profusely. How he wished he could just unwrap his coat and throw it below, but he couldn't; the ammunition was in its pockets, and it also protected him from the worst of the cold.

It was only then that Creighton began to realise the general's dream. Of course, the elite sharpshooter needs a warm but relatively lightweight coat both to protect him and to allow mobility in awkward positions. Rule number one had been laid down – in his mind.

Creighton took aim at the bucket, but the gun wavered in the breeze. He tried to pull the rifle more tightly to his shoulder, but still it swung. He then pulled the shoulder strap in the opposite direction to the movement of the gun and ship and nearly lost his footing. He took his time, made himself comfortable again, carefully lining up the front sight with the rear blade. He thought again about distance and wind, compensated and fired.

He ripped a hole in the deck.

'Careful of my ship!' the captain roared.

'Try again!' the general roared even louder.

The only roaring Creighton could hear was from sea, wind and rifle, but strangely this made him more focused, for they were natural elements that didn't necessarily work against him. They were predictable in their vehemence, so he let himself become a part of them, to sway with the motion of the ship, to accept the driving wind and cold, to assess the strength of windage, continually – but only fractionally – adjusting his position. And then, on his second shot, he punched a hole in the bucket.

'Good show!' bellowed the general. 'Again!'

Creighton knew what the general was thinking. Was it a lucky shot? He tried to re-enact the procedure exactly as he'd done it before, but he did it slowly, he took his time... and he missed.

No. He knew he'd done it right. It *felt* right. He adjusted himself, settled down again, went with the flow and then fired. He hit the bucket again. Then he did it again, and again.

Eventually he threw the rifle over his shoulder and started to descend. He couldn't feel his fingers now, apart from the one that had been pulling the trigger, which felt slightly stiff. It took him a full five minutes to return to the deck. The general met him and slapped him powerfully on the back. 'You see? It worked! By gad, we're going to give those Union boys a whipping.'

Creighton cracked a smile, albeit a short-lived one as the general thought of a new torture. 'We must approach the enemy from different angles, Creighton. I suggest we both try to shoot the Ferrell from the top of the flag at the stern of the ship whilst lying prostrate at the other end. Remember, it must be achieved in one shot for the element of surprise. Although in battle more than one shot can be achieved, you can achieve prime-target opportunity once and once only.'

The torture continued, not just for a few hours but for days and days, but the training was paying off. Both Creighton and the general could see the improvements, could analyse and document the correct format, to prepare mentally, to control their breathing, knowing exactly when to breathe. Yes, they had stumbled upon an art form, and because they were its innovators, they buried themselves in the work, even pressing the wives and crew to join them. Suddenly the general found himself leading a crack team of sharpshooters.

Creighton kept a log – 'The Sharpshooters' Bible', he would later call it, by Creighton and Saunderson. What he and the general had stumbled upon wasn't just innovation; it was a whole new science.

'Ship astern!' came a throaty cry.

The crew and passengers ran to the side of the ship, eager to ascertain whether the newcomer was friend or foe. An uneasy feeling passed through the company. The ship that approached was a relatively new paddle steamer, while the general's ship was a reconditioned frigate from the Napoleonic War, converted into a haven for contraband and little else. However, there were two cannon and four portals – two on either side of the upper deck. The captain signalled for the cannons to be made ready and trained on the approaching vessel. It wasn't long before the ship was angling up alongside them.

'Where are you bound for, friend?' came a cry in an American accent.

'South America,' the captain replied in a well-rehearsed manner. 'To Venezuela?'

'Aye, we are that,' replied the captain, but the end of his sentence was lost in the whiz of cannon fire.

'The colours!' the captain shouted. 'Strike the colours!'

Saunderson had placed the British flag at the stern, and the giveaway was obvious. The first explosion blew the first cannon bay to bits, killing a sailor who was leaving his post to strike the colours.

'Attack!' screamed Saunderson, but the second sailor had left his post and raced to escape in the ship's long boat, which had been fitted primarily for the ladies' benefit. Saunderson was having none of it; the man was a deserter and had to be punished.

The second explosion blew the main sail down, killing the captain and the first mate outright. Saunderson locked with his deserter and was given a bloody nose for his trouble. Turning away, he faced the navigator, who was holding a cutlass high above his head, but before even the most nimble could move, half of the navigator's face fell to the floor in a bloody mess and his lifeless torso fell into the hold.

Sharpshooters! Saunderson thought. *They have their own sharpshooters!* Instinctively he peered through the gunsmoke to ascertain where the shots had come from and took a shot directly in the middle of his forehead. He was dead before he hit the floor.

Creighton and the remaining sailor got the long boat into the water and the women over the side and safely into it. There was a crunch of timber as another cannonball struck behind them. Creighton froze for a moment and then, bewildered, turned around and made his way through the gunsmoke, searching for the general.

'Creighton! Come on!' called Florence, as Lady Saunderson pushed the oars through the futtocks and desperately tried to row the boat away.

'Come on, Florence! You must help me!'

'But, Creighton!' she wailed.

'He'll come. Now help me move this boat to safety.'

Florence did her best to comply.

As the smoke cleared, Creighton saw General Saunderson's corpse and fell heavily to his knees – and it was that one simple act that saved his life. As he fell, he twisted his body and the shot fired at his chest tore through his shoulder cleanly. It felt as if he'd been struck by a white-hot poker strapped to a swinging hammer. He screamed out in pain, but at the same time he was snapped out of his trance: the general was dead, the ship lost, the crew murdered. But the women?

Creighton quickly scrambled to his feet and ran to starboard. Without a second's hesitation, he jumped over the side and into the deep blue sea. As he fell, he felt a musket ball blow the heel off his shoe. *By God, they're great sharpshooters*, he thought as he plummeted, a vision of the last sailor dead on the deck burned in his mind.

Once in the water, he thrashed around, gasping for breath, but he soon realised he was drowning. The sea had no bottom. Momentarily he relaxed, pushed up with his chest, his arms arcing in front of him, the pain screaming through his shoulder, causing him to grit his teeth, his mouth distended in a rictus of agony.

At last, he gasped sweet air. Glancing around him, he caught the silhouette of the long boat, making poor progress on the open sea no more than 200 yards in front of him, and struck out for it. He splashed his arms and legs to give him momentum, but the pain tore through him and he nearly sank below the waves. He gritted his teeth and pushed on, tears mingling with the already salty water. It was only then that Creighton realised the plumes of red spreading around him – his life's blood!

The wound in his shoulder was gaping, aggravated by salt water and the violence of his thrashing arms. Surely there was nothing left but to give up, to surrender to the sea. But something gave him hope: his total fear of the creature whose fin came cutting through the water towards him.

Shark!

Thankfully, only one. *Thankfully?*

Creighton lashed out with his good arm and smacked the enormous fish on the tip of its nose, and it instantly ducked away.

Creighton realised he was in open water again, swept to the left – away from the long boat – by the waves.

'Come on, Creighton!' Florence pleaded, stretching her hands towards him. 'Come on!' But then her pleading gave way to a terrifying scream.

Creighton couldn't see what was coming up behind him, but he had a good idea. Instinctively he kicked upwards, his whole body wrenching as he did so. As he screamed out, an iron grip caught him by the foot and dragged him down into the depths of the ocean.

In the long boat, Florence looked out over a suddenly peaceful blue-and-red sea and the nearby carcass of a smoking ship. Lady Saunders had turned back to the act of rowing, her eyes haunted.

Trembling, Florence turned and, instead of begging Lady Saunders to stay, to help her look for her husband, sat down and took up the oars. She was keen to be gone.

As soon as she did so, a hand gripped the side of the boat. Both ladies yelped.

'Help me.'

It was a wasted man's voice, but it was definitely Creighton. The two ladies got up and pulled him into the boat. He was shivering with pain and exertion. 'For the love of God, surrender,' he gritted through clenched teeth. 'You'll both die out here. Just surrender. Save yourselves, I'm already dead.'

At this, Florence regained some of her old composure. 'Oh, Creighton, do stop. You're only concerned for yourself. I mean, I'm not wearing the right outfit to surrender.'

Creighton closed his eyes and awaited a fate worse than death.

Afterword

'If we shadows have offended,
Think but this and all is mended.'

WILLIAM SHAKESPEARE, *A MIDSUMMER NIGHT'S DREAM*

The anatomy of a sniper is a complex thing to study, largely because there are many different types of sniper – those who fight for good, mercenaries, professionals, amateurs. Many of these suffer poor representations in books and cinema, but likewise many are portrayed realistically both on screen and in print.

The sniper is an intriguing figure because he is unseen, like the monster that hides under a young child's bed.

In this book, we've attempted to explain some of the most famous – and intricate – sniper action of the past 200 years, after speaking to people directly involved with sniping in real-life situations and studying their fictional counterparts. We hope that you've now been informed as to what a true sniper is, and how he does have a place on the battlefield, working for the good of the free world.

Perhaps in a hundred years' time the sniper will no longer be a viable tool of battle, because his covert situations can be pinpointed and his lair destroyed from a distance. Indeed, this can be partially achieved today. Sniping is a point in time, part of the human race's bloody history, and here we've tried to document the sniping aspect of that history.

Don't have nightmares.

Craig Cabell and Richard Brown
London, July 2005

Glossary of Firearms Terms

We decided that it might be a useful exercise to produce a firearms glossary for any readers who aren't familiar with military and ballistic terminology. Not all these terms are used in the book, but if the reader wishes to explore the subject further, this list should help. The list has been based on a generic glossary supplied by the US National Rifle Association, but we've furnished our own definitions for a more global readership and added some specific terms on sniping. The list is by no means fully comprehensive, but it will enable the beginner to use terms with a degree of authority!

ACTION: The moving parts in a firearm that operate the firing of the round. Many types of action have been used throughout history, the most common being single-shot, multi-barrel, revolvers, slide-action or pump-action, lever-action, bolt-action, semi-automatic and fully automatic.

AIRGUN: A gun that resembles a gunpowder firearm but uses compressed air or CO_2 to propel a lead pellet down a barrel. Airguns come in .177, .20, .22 and .25 calibres and can take the form of either rifle or pistol. They have little range or accuracy when compared to gunpowder weapons, but they offer excellent accuracy at ranges of less than 50m.

AMMUNITION: For the purposes of this book, the term 'ammunition' primarily refers to a complete modern round – that is, a bullet, brass (or metallic) cartridge, powder and primer. It can also be used as a term for inert lead balls – shot – fired from muzzle-loading guns and for airgun pellets.

ASSAULT RIFLE: For the purposes of this book, this term refers to a modern (i.e. post-Second World War) rifle capable of semi-automatic and, sometimes, fully automatic fire. It's different from a sub-machine gun in that it fires rifle ammunition rather than pistol ammunition. Most assault rifles are calibred in 5.56mm or 7.62mm, although several other calibres are easily available and have been used historically. The first true assault rifle was the MP44, which appeared late in the Second World War. Had the German Army had this weapon earlier in the war, some battles might have had different outcomes. Notable examples of assault rifles are the AK47, M16, SA80 and G3.

AUTOMATIC PISTOL: A misnomer applied to a pistol equipped with a magazine that feeds rounds, loads and then ejects spent cases. The term has now become so ingrained in the gun world that even purists can find themselves using it in moments of weakness. The correct term for such a weapon is *self-loading pistol*.

BALL: This word originally referred to the lead balls fired from black-powder guns. It is a term which has stayed with us, however, and is now used to describe round-nosed bullets, especially metal-jacket rounds used by armed forces.

BIPOD: A two-legged support fitted to the front of a rifle and which is designed to support the weapon and make eye/scope relief easier.

BLACK POWDER: The earliest type of firearms propellant that has now been replaced by a mix of nitro-glycerine and nitro-cellulose powder, which converts to gas rather than burns. Black powder is now used only by enthusiasts of muzzle-loading guns who shoot antique weapons. In the UK, government authority is often required for the use of black powder, as it is considered an explosive.

BLANK CARTRIDGE: A brass case in a specific calibre loaded with gunpowder but crimped and sealed at the end (i.e. without a bullet). Blanks are often used to start races, in theatrical or film productions, and in troop exercises and training.

BOLT ACTION: This term describes a rifle mechanism that's activated by the shooter manually operating the breech block. The process of the bolt action loads a cartridge and, after firing, ejects the spent case. The gun can be cycled only as quickly as the shooter can operate the mechanism.

BORE: The interior of a firearm's barrel, excluding the chamber.

BULLET: The actual projectile that is fired from the gun. The bullet is an element of ammunition (see above).

CALIBRE: The diameter of the bore of a gun, measured as part of an inch (e.g. .38) or in millimetres (e.g. 9mm). The calibre of the bullet to be fired from the gun matches almost perfectly the calibre of the bore, but is actually a little larger than the bore to allow for a tight fit in the barrel and for some of the bullet to be shaved off by the rifling of the gun.

CARBINE: A rifle with a shorter barrel than the standard infantry model. Carbines were originally created for mounted troops, who found the full-length infantry gun too long for effective use on horseback. Carbines are now favoured weapons in urban and close-quarter battle situations.

CARTRIDGE: A complete round, comprising ammunition, case, powder, bullet and primer. The term also refers to a complete shotgun shell. (See the entry for *ammunition*.)

CHAMBER: 1. The rear part of the barrel of a rifle or semi-/fully automatic weapon that's specially shaped to accept a cartridge. 2. A charge hold in a revolver cylinder. Into each of these – typically six in number – a complete round is placed.

CLIP: A slang term for the removable magazine placed within a gun to deliver bullets. In pistols, the clip is traditionally stored within the pistol grip, while in rifles the clip is usually in front of the trigger unit.

DUM-DUM BULLET: A bullet developed for the British military in India's Dum-Dum Arsenal and used on the country's northwest frontier and in the Sudan in 1897 and 1898. It took the form of a jacketed .303-calibre bullet with the jacket nose left open to expose the lead core in the hope of increasing effectiveness. Its use was discontinued following the Hague Convention of 1899, which outlawed the use of such bullets in warfare. Often the term 'dum-

dum' is misapplied to any soft-nosed or hollow-point hunting bullet (see chapter two).

FIRING PIN: The part of a gun that strikes the primer of a bullet, igniting it. The firing pin is either held back by a spring or struck by an external hammer.

FLASH HIDER/SUPPRESSOR: A framework device attachment designed to reduce muzzle flash caused by the burning of excess propellant as the bullet leaves the barrel. This is a very important device, especially for the sniper, as the muzzle flash of a gun can give away his position. Indeed, any muzzle flash is ballistically undesirable, as it shows that not all of the charge has combusted behind the bullet and so some energy has been lost.

FLYER: A stray round that ends up nowhere near the target when all other shots in the batch were on target. Flyers can be caused by environmental conditions or a poorly manufactured round.

FULLY AUTOMATIC: A fully automatic weapon will continue to fire as long as the user engages the trigger.

GUNPOWDER: A black, granular, explosive substance consisting of an intimate mechanical mixture of 70 to 80 per cent nitre and 10 to 15 per cent each of charcoal and sulphur. Its explosive energy is considerable due to the fact that it contains the necessary amount of oxygen for its own combustion and liberates gases (chiefly nitrogen and carbon dioxide) that occupy 1,000 or 1,500 times more space than the powder which generated them.

HANDGUN: Another name for a pistol or revolver. This term is used only with regard to a weapon that can be held and fired accurately with one hand.

HIGH-CAPACITY MAGAZINE: A relatively new term that came along at the same time as the 'wonder nines', or 9mm self-loading pistols, which hold up to fifteen rounds in each magazine. The invention of double-stacking magazines doubled overnight the number of rounds that a handgun could take. The existence of high-capacity magazines has often been noted as a factor in falling shooting standards, as the shooter can now 'spray and pray' rather than concentrate on a well-aimed shot.

HOLLOW-POINT BULLET: A bullet whose tip has been hollowed out to aid expansion on impact. Hollow-point rounds find great favour with law-enforcement units, who require maximum impact transfer to the target with minimum penetration. Military users, on the other hand, prefer ball ammunition (see above), which is more likely to penetrate body armour. The best mix is for the hollow point of the round to be made of soft lead and the rear section to be jacketed, which will maintain the structural integrity of the bullet on impact.

IRON SIGHTS: The metal sights that come as standard on all modern guns, to be used in lieu of any additional optical sighting.

JACKET: The invention of jackets on rounds came about primarily due to the invention of self-loading weapons. The process of jacketing involves covering the lead bullet with a metal (commonly copper) cover, or jacket. The jacket has two purposes, the first of which is to aid the loading process. Lead is a very soft metal, and if you're firing rapidly with a semi-automatic weapon there's always a chance that a lead bullet will deform as it's rammed into the breech. The copper jacket prevents this. It also helps maintain the physical integrity of the round on impact with the target.

LEVER ACTION: This term refers to an alternative method of cycling ammunition to bolt-action. Most common in guns of a Winchester style, lever-action mechanisms were truly the first effective at loading and ejecting rounds in a multi-shot rifle. The mechanism is fairly reliable as, like that of a bolt-action gun, the shooter's own hand movement cycles the gun. The lever is actually part of the hand guard under the rifle. This is dropped, which allows the feeding of the first round out of the magazine. As the lever is pulled back up to the stock, the round is pushed into battery. After firing, the process is repeated. The initial dropping of the lever also ejects the fired case.

MACHINE GUN: A term used to describe a gun that is more crew-operated than fired by one person. A machine gun is a fully automatic long weapon used for support and suppression purposes. It will fire a rifle round of high power and is often fed by a belt of bullets, which are guided into the side of the gun by a second operator.

MAGAZINE: A spring-loaded container that takes the shape of a long (often curved) box and which holds cartridges. Magazines are often inserted into the framework of a gun – for example, into the pistol grip of a handgun. They're high-precision pieces of equipment and have been designed to feed round after round, and can be reloaded hundreds of time before problems occur with feeding rounds into the breech.

The existence of the detachable magazine also allows for quick loading. In self-loading pistols, magazines can hold anything from six to eighteen rounds, depending on the gun, while magazines designed for use with sub-machine guns can hold between fifteen and forty rounds, while some specialist models hold fifty.

Other magazines are not detachable but are instead an integral party of the gun, possibly taking the form of a second tube under the barrel. Rounds are pushed into these and are fed back into the breech via spring pressure and the action of the gun shooting.

MAGNUM: A term indicating a heavily loaded metallic cartridge or shot shell, although the term is also applied to the gun that fires this cartridge – for example, the .357 Magnum bullets can be fired out of the Smith & Wesson Distinguished Combat Magnum revolver. Magnum rounds are high-powered loads that don't always lend themselves well to comfortable shooting. They were traditionally fired only by revolvers and some rifles, but now they're available in semi-automatic pistols, such as the Desert Eagle. The visual impact of these guns – which is impressive – had sadly led to them becoming not just a fine combat handgun but also a status symbol in the criminal world.

MULTI-BARRELLED: A term used to describe a gun with more than one barrel, the most common example of which is the double-barrel shotgun. Some military weapons are now multi-barrelled, including the Vulcan Minigun, which is commonly mounted to helicopters and vehicles and has six barrels which revolve, taking a round from a magazine in turn, making for fast firing and limited barrel wear.

MUZZLE: The open end of the barrel from which the projectile exits.

MUZZLE BRAKE: An attachment to a weapon's barrel – most commonly that of a rifle – that bleeds off escaping combustion gasses in specific directions in order to reduce the recoil of the weapon. In a pistol, for example, some gas behind the bullet is vented out and up in order to push the barrel down.

MUZZLE LOADER: This term refers to the oldest type of guns – i.e. those that were used prior to the invention of the metal cartridge – which are still very popular with shooting enthusiasts today. The principle is explained in some detail in chapter two, but essentially their loading procedure involves pushing the gunpowder and ball manually into the gun from the muzzle. This gunpowder is then ignited to fire the round.

NIGHT-VISION SCOPE: A variation of the sniper scope that gathers all available light during night operations and magnifies it. The image is often green or black and white. Very modern sniper scopes can be equipped with day/night scopes that can toggle between light and dark modes at the flick of a switch.

PELLETS: Small spherical projectiles loaded into shot shells and more often known as 'shot'. The term is also applied generically to airgun ammunition.

PISTOL: A generic term used for any gun that can be aimed and fired with the hand. The term is nowadays more applicable to a self-loading weapon rather than a revolver.

PRIMER: The ignition component of a cartridge (i.e. the part of the cartridge which is hit by the firing pin to make a spark), composed of metallic fulminate or lead styphnate.

RANGE FINDER: A device commonly used by long-range shooters and troops gathering intelligence for artillery divisions.

Such a device looks a little like a standard pair of binoculars but actually fires a laser at the target and calculates its distance, displaying this and the direction of the target in the viewing lens. A typical readout would be '787M – 63°'.

RECEIVER: The part of a firearm in which the loading and firing mechanism is stored – for example, a telescopic sight on a sniper rifle is fitted to the top of the receiver.

RETICLE: The crosshairs of a sniper scope. These come in various forms, such as the traditional cross and a T shape, as discussed in annexe A. Most modern sniper reticles have many marks to help the shooter judge the range of the target.

REVOLVER: A gun (normally a handgun) with a multi-chambered cylinder (typically containing six shots) that rotates in order that each chamber can be successively aligned with a single barrel and firing pin.

RIFLE: A shoulder-fired gun with a rifled bore.

RIFLING: Spiral grooves cut into a barrel to impart spin on the travelling bullet. The shape of the rifling is unique to each gun and leaves a mark as individual as a fingerprint on the bullet. The high part of the rifling is called the *land* and the low part is called the *groove*.

ROUND: Another name for a single, complete cartridge. It can also be applied to the bullet after it has left the gun.

SELECTIVE FIRE: A function on a weapon whereby the shooter can select for the weapon to fire semi-automatically (i.e. one round for each pull of the trigger) or fully automatically (i.e. the weapon continues to fire as long as the trigger is held down).

SEMI-AUTOMATIC: A term used to describe a firearm designed to fire a single cartridge, then eject the empty case and reload the chamber each time the trigger is pulled. This operation is achieved by harnessing the huge pressure behind the bullet, which is used to activate a spring-locked mechanism.

SHOTGUN: A shoulder-fired gun with a smooth-bored barrel (or barrels) designed primarily for firing multiple small, round projectiles encased in a plastic shell. Some shotgun barrels are rifled in order to give better accuracy.

SHOT SHELL: A cartridge for a shotgun, also called simply a *shell*. The body of a shot shell may be of metal and plastic or of plastic and paper, and has a metal head. The projectile actually comprises several small lead balls, which spread apart on leaving the gun.

SIGHTS: See *iron sights* and *telescopic sight*.

SILENCER: A slang term for a suppressor (see below).

SINGLE-SHOT: A term that describes a gun – very commonly, airguns – with a chamber in which separately carried rounds must be manually placed one at a time.

SLUG: A slang but oft-used term for a bullet after flight, particularly after it has hit the target.

SMOOTH BORE: A term that describes a gun with a barrel that bears no rifling.

STOCK: The wooden or plastic furniture surrounding a rifle's mechanism.

SUB-MACHINE GUN: A small weapon capable of fully automatic fire and which almost always fires pistol ammunition, although there are some exceptions. Sub-machine guns are short-range weapons (100m to a maximum of 150m) used primarily for suppression purposes and assaults on buildings and are poorly suited to the wide, open areas of the battlefield due to the limitations imposed by their ammunition.

SUPPRESSOR: A device that can be fitted to any gun and is designed to suppress the noise of a firing round. No self-loading or fully automatic gun can ever be fully silenced, as there will always be the sound of the bolt or slide moving. The device works by trapping gases, which reduces the sound and velocity of the round. Nevertheless, if the bullet still leaves the gun at supersonic speed, there will be a loud crack, whereas the use of subsonic ammunition greatly reduces the noise of the gun.

SUSTAINED FIRE: See *fully automatic*.

TELESCOPIC SIGHT: An optical aid that provides a magnified image of the target, like a telescope. Having a telescopic sight fitted to the top of a gun greatly enhances the shooter's accuracy. Such a device obviously doesn't make a bullet any more powerful, but it does enable the shooter to aim well beyond the range of the human eye.

ZERO: To calibrate a gun's sights to a set distance (i.e. 100m).

Further Reading

The technical data used in this book was cross-referenced from the following volumes. (Please note that each edition used for reference purposes is the copy acknowledged and recommended for further reading.)

BEATTY, WILLIAM, MD: *The Death Of Lord Nelson –*
21 October 1805 (*War Library*, edited and published by Prof Edward Arber, FSA)
The Memoirs Of Field-Marshal Montgomery (Collins, 1958)
Clint Eastwood Interviews (Mississippi, 1999)
CACUTT, LEN (editor): *Combat* (Guild Publishing, 1998)
FLEMING, IAN: *The Living Daylights* (Jonathan Cape, 1966, containing the novels *Octopussy* and *The Living Daylights*)
FORSYTH, FREDERICK: *The Day Of The Jackal* (Hutchinson, 1971)
FORSYTH, FREDERICK: *The Odessa File* (Hutchinson, 1972)
GILBERT, ADRIAN: *Sniper: One On One* (Pan Books, 1994)

GUTZMAN, PHILIP: *Vietnam* (PRC, 2002)

HARTNIK, A: *The Complete Encyclopedia of Army Automatic Rifles* (Rebo Publishing, 1999)

MARKHAM, GEORGE: *Guns Of The Reich* (Arms & Armour Press, 1989)

MOOSE, CHARLES: *Three Weeks In October: The Hunt For The Washington Sniper* (Orion, 2004)

MYATT, MAJ F, MC: *Modern Small Arms* (Salamander, 1978)

MYATT, MAJ F, MC: *19th Century Firearms* (Tiger Books, 1979)

PEGLER, MARTIN: *Powder & Ball Small Arms* (Corwood Press, 1998)

REMARQUE, ERICH MARIA: *All Quiet On The Western Front* (Vintage, 1996)

ROBBINS, DAVID L: *War Of The Rats* (Orion, 1999)

ROBBINS, DAVID L: *The End Of War* (Orion, 2000)

SMITH & SMITH: *Small Arms Of The World* (Galahad Publishing, 1973)

SOUTHEY, ROBERT: *The Life Of Nelson* (Folio Society, 1956)

SPICER, MARK: *Sniper* (Salamander, 2001)

Back issues of the following magazines, newspapers and journals were also consulted:

Arms & Explosives magazine (November 1908)

Book & Magazine Collector (December 2004)

Book & Magazine Collector (Christmas 2004)

Guns & Ammo magazine (Pirmedia Publishing)

Gun Mart (Aceville Magazines, 2001)

Rifle magazine (no. 276 in pattern 1914 [1913])

The Times (13 May 1863)

Photo Credits and Copyright